Is my wonderf [handwritten note]

Catherine Wallace is Professor Emerita at University College London, Institute of Education. This is her first book that can be broadly described as creative non-fiction. Her other publications are in her academic field of Applied Linguistics and Literacy Education and include books for learners of English as a Foreign Language.

from Cathie [handwritten note]

Orchard Stories

CATHERINE WALLACE

The manufacturer's authorised representative in the EU for product safety is Authorised Rep
Compliance Ltd, 71 Lower Baggot Street, Dublin D02 P593 Ireland
(www.arccompliance.com)

Troubador Publishing Ltd
Unit E2 Airfield Business Park
Harrison Road, Market Harborough
Leicestershire LE16 7UL
Tel: 0116 279 2299
Email: books@troubador.co.uk
Web: www.troubador.co.uk

ISBN 978-1-83628-173-3

British Library Cataloguing in Publication Data.
A catalogue record for this book is available from the British Library.

Printed and bound in Great Britain by 4edge Limited
Typeset in 11pt Minion Pro by Troubador Publishing Ltd, Leicester, UK

This book is dedicated to my friends and neighbours at The Orchard. This is their story and could not have been told without their kindness, cooperation and good humour.

Special thanks are also due to those who agreed to be interviewed or gave permission for their voices to be recorded.* They are:

Jackie Fryer
James Galbraith
Luca Gianandrea
Gergő and Balint Imre
Emil Kowalski
Joe O'Moricue
Andrzej Sikorski
Eszter Virt
Emma Williams

*In some cases pseudonyms are used

CONTENTS

PREFACE

Certain parts of London, more distinct and picturesque than others, are known as 'villages'. Hampstead and Richmond would be examples. Ealing in West London, despite being dubbed 'Queen of the Suburbs', on account of its leafy streets and parks, struggles to claim this identity. It is village-like in parts but also very much town: to be precise, seven towns: Ealing, Hanwell, Perivale, Greenford, Southall, Northolt and Acton. A tranquil, settled community in its 'leafier' parts coexists with a poorer population living in rundown streets at the further reaches of the borough.

The block of flats at the centre of my stories shares this precarious identity. Built in the 1930s, it would originally have housed rather well-heeled citizens, pillars of the community even. But in more recent years it has taken on some of the transitoriness of a metropolis. Flat dwellers tend anyway to be different from those who live in semi-detached family houses. There is an unsought cohabitation, the muttering of 'hellos', as we sidle pass each other in shared spaces. A grudging acquaintance with some of our neighbours, but otherwise a comfortable anonymity.

But then came 'lockdown'. A word previously barely heard of became not only a central part of our vocabulary, but a new lived reality.

So it was that in March 2020 this thing called 'lockdown' brought a fresh perspective to life at The Orchard. In enforced seclusion we became both more distant from each other but also more interdependent. And more curious as to who we would be sharing our lives with in the uncertain months ahead.

Lockdown invited attention both to the micro world of The Orchard, but also to the wider context of what came to be a global pandemic. Along with a thousand households across the land, I wished to document a changed way of life, with its new rhythms, contradictions, and fears. But I also aimed to situate these few rather dramatic years within a larger, more ordinary slice of life – my long stay at The Orchard, now over forty years. I wanted to capture the comings and goings: those who stay and those who leave. Stability and yet restlessness.

My stories come in three sections.

Part one starts with the early lockdown days but then takes a detour to move back in time to the eighties, to my early days at The Orchard.

Part two returns us to the immediate situation of lockdown, as it becomes clear that we are in this for the long haul, that what we thought was a brief interruption in our daily lives has moved into a more settled modus vivendi.

The final, shorter section brings the stories up to date. In what ways has the pandemic impacted on lives both at The Orchard and beyond? What lies ahead for my Orchard characters? For the people who have become a closer part of my life than in the earlier years.

Retired as a lecturer in applied linguistics, I was interested in language as an element of what we might call the Covid experience: what language did we use to make sense of this sudden upheaval in our lives? But also the language directed at us, whether calculated to reassure or to persuade and cajole. Was the goal to represent material reality, as fully and fairly as possible? Or to distort and obfuscate?

There's a lot about language and politics in these stories, reflecting not just my own interests but those of many Orchard folk – Orchardians, as I came to call them. Hungry for human contact, whenever there was a pause in Covid constraints, we talked – and we talked politics. For many of us, the personal and the political came together. How did we make sense of the new world in which we found ourselves? A world that was struggling not just with the pandemic, but with Brexit, and, later, the war in Ukraine.

Within these broader preoccupations, the minutiae of daily life in a block of flats played out. What had previously been taken for granted came under closer scrutiny. We noticed each other more. With time on our hands – as well as having a constant eye on the 'world out there' – we turned attention inwards. And I was one of many who responded to the Covid crisis by keeping a diary to track this new day-to-day flow of events.

Some Orchard characters make a fleeting appearance; others are threaded through all sections of the stories. I came to think of the earlier residents, myself included, as the 'Old-Timers' while the new kids on the block became known as the 'New Cosmopolitans'.

Now life has settled and we are going about our everyday business, much as we did before. The feeling of unease is dissipating. There is still, however, a sense that things will not ever be quite the same.

I took the opportunity of lockdown to talk to and record my Orchard neighbours, always with their permission. So in the stories which relate to the present day and recent past, their accounts are woven into my own observations and my daily diary entries. In the case of the Old-Timers I depend on my own memories and of those who shared their lives with them during earlier days at The Orchard.

As one of my characters says of another, with a particularly colourful – and at times barely credible past – 'it's all true'. This is the case here. In places I have changed names and flat numbers to offer my Orchard friends and neighbours some privacy. Otherwise these are their stories. And my own stories also. And they are all, by and large, true.

PRINCIPLE CHARACTERS

Early years at The Orchard (1981 to 2000):

Flat six: *Nancy Taylor*. An elderly widow. Suffers from deafness and ulcerated legs. Unfailingly cheerful and courteous. As a young woman had been Princess Elizabeth's hairdresser, joining her on the trip to Kenya, where the princess learnt of her father's death.

Flat nine: *Tom Moynihan*. A colleague at Ealing Technical College. Moves out within a few years to be replaced by another tech lecturer, American *Gary Hoffman*.

Flat ten: *Saoirse O'Brien*. Of Irish background. Teacher of home economics at a local comprehensive school. Arrives shortly after me in the early '80s, before taking early retirement and moving to the West Country to be near her mother.

Flat twelve: *Cathie Wallace (me)*.

Flat thirteen: *James Galbraith*. From a Northern Irish family. Moves into the flat in the late '80s, after it is repossessed by bailiffs. James's sister *Hazel* and her husband *Jack* with their two little girls are also Orchard dwellers for a few years, first in flat seven and then in flat five, before leaving to pursue their careers as artists in the South of France.

Flat fourteen: *Gerald and Jeanne Horrocks.* Preparatory schoolmaster, Gerald, with his French wife Jeanne, takes on much of the running of Orchard finances for some years, later moving to a detached house in a neighbouring street.

Flat fifteen: *Diana Smythe.* A cultured woman, once a renowned writer, now with dementia. She owns a vicious dog.

Flat sixteen: an old man whose name I never discover – later replaced by *Jan Bukowski*, a taciturn Pole, celebrated by his community as a cavalryman who served with considerable bravery in the Second World War.

Flat eighteen: *Holda and Dack Fryer.* In their seventies when I arrive at The Orchard. A charming, handsome couple, each with roots in Ealing.

The millennium and beyond (2000 to 2020):

Flat five: *Anna Jurgis* and *Armando Ferreira* move to The Orchard around the turn of the new century. Armando, Portuguese, good-looking, athletic; always rushing off on his bike. Does something big in IT and is my first port of call for techie support. Anna works for the Arts Council of Great Britain.

Flat six: for several years there are families with two sets of twins, first boys and then girls, followed by two primary schoolteachers. I come to call them the Wild Girls. Demure during the day but famous for frenzied parties at the weekend. Once the schoolteachers move on, *Becky* and *Leonard Jennings* arrive with their sons, *Olly* and *Matt.*

Flat seven: *Hanna Novak.* Born in Poland. Lives with her boyfriend, *Ziggy.* Flat seven sees a lot of coming and going, from drug dealers in the early days to – much later, post-Covid – a charming thirty-something Filipino surgeon called *Darrell Barcelona*. Darrell is later joined by his wife *Samantha* and son *Jarvis*.

Flat eight: *Joe O'Moricue*. Went to art school in Australia. A talented and prolific painter but also turns his hand in hard times to painting and decorating.

Flat ten: *Jannis Turner*. An archivist at one of London's universities. Sweet, polite and pleasant when we pass in the corridor but tends to avoid socialising.

Flat fourteen: *Emil Kowalski*. Tall and urbane, I call him 'Emil the banker', though that doesn't really capture a career spent troubleshooting for various organisations across the Middle East. Often has his glamorous mother *Barbara* to stay with him.

Flat seventeen: *Harold* and *Eileen Sinclair*. The perfect, considerate neighbours. Now mostly based in Norfolk, which has been their main home for some time.

Flat eighteen: *Elena Edwards* buys the flat after Holda Fryer dies. After a succession of Elena's itinerant tenants, who come and go with rapidity, *Herve* and *Lupita*, with their son *Matteus*, move in. They leave not long before lockdown

The lockdown years (2020 to 2023):

Flat three: Italians, *Luca Gianandrea* with friends *Riccardo and Valentina* – whose surnames I never discover – and a boy, *Lorenzo*. The two men work in the restaurant business. Valentina takes care of Lorenzo.

Flat six: just a few weeks in advance of Covid, a Hungarian family arrives: *Eszter Virt* and *Tamás Imre* and their boys *Gergő* and *Balint*.

Flat eleven: *Bart* and *Emma Williams*. Bart is a

Vietnamese Australian, adopted as a child from Saigon, an experience he describes in his book *But What are You?*. Bart does stunt work in films, along with straight acting when he gets the chance. He also leads online fitness classes for The Orchard community during lockdown. Emma is a senior executive for a pharmaceutical company. They have a Hungarian pointer called *Darius*.

Flat thirteen: just before Covid, *James Galbraith* is joined by his partner, later wife, whose African name is *Chansa* but who's also known as *Simone*. James runs a charity called The Book Bus which supports literacy in developing countries, working much of the time in Zambia where he met Simone, employed by the same charity. The Book Bus is often parked at the back of The Orchard behind the garages.

Flat eighteen: *Basabdatta Ghosh, Anirban Chel* and their little boy *Arin*. Originally from India. Both very successful in IT. Arin is a star footballer at the local primary school.

Flat nineteen: *Irene Magne*. A dramatic Russian, briefly succeeded the mysterious *Peter* the Slovakian. Now Irene has gone with her boyfriend to Watford, to be replaced, just as lockdown is announced, by a beautiful young Indian couple.

Flat twenty: *Chikayo Hirito.* Teaches at the Japanese School in Ealing. Known for her charm and her terrible driving. Speaks little English as the Japanese School in Ealing makes its teachers work such long days that the mainly Japanese staff barely have time to socialise. Chikayo leaves mid-lockdown to be replaced by *Ivan Petrov*, Bulgarian, married to *Maggie*, who is Polish. They have two little girls, *Octavia* and *Clara*.

The visitors:

Andrzej Sikorski (sometimes known as Andrew). Though not a resident, Andrzej is a major player in the affairs of The Orchard, owning two of the flats and serving as President of the Residents Association. Keeps his treasured vintage cars carefully secured in two garages out the back, just by The Book Bus.

Wendy and *Jackie Fryer.* Dack's daughters. Regular visitors since the 1970s, first to Dack and Holda's flat and subsequently to flat twelve. Keen gardeners and sharp observers of change at The Orchard, which, in general, they deplore.

Noel Greig. Playwright, gay activist and actor. My boyfriend in our university days, later best friend, an honorary Orchardian until his death in 2009.

Ian Rogers. Keyboard player who shares the running of our book group, known as 'Bookbreak', in Ladbroke Grove. Leaves his piano in my flat when evicted from his place in Kilburn – after nearly thirty years.

Kim Thorne. Acts as an odd-job man around The Orchard between 2015 and 2018. During those years, he is to be found almost daily in a shed in the garden.

Una Dinning. Writer and painter. Lives in Cambridgeshire but a frequent visitor to number twelve.

Brzoska Shannon. Originally from Poland but has lived in the UK for many years. Cleans for me and occasionally for Emil at number fourteen. She also works in a high-end London fashion store. Always tastefully dressed, Brzoska is the most elegant member of The Orchard community.

PROLOGUE

A large brick building set back from the street, it could be an old school house or a downmarket hotel. The Orchard has no distinguishing features, apart from the shabby canopy over the front door which says simply THE ORCHARD. It was the seedy façade along with the noir-ish feel of the long Orchard corridors that had prompted the director for the *Inspector Morse* series to film an episode here. Called 'Driven to Distraction', it features a deranged driving instructor who murders rather a lot of women in West London.

The Orchard stands at the edge of the conservation area known as the Brentham Estate – one of the earliest garden suburbs and an inspiration for the later, larger and more famous Hampstead Garden Suburb. Coming from Ealing Broadway, you strike across Haven Green and make your way up Mount Park Road, with its confident-looking, solid Victorian houses, some maintaining the look of comfortable family homes, while others have the more uncertain mien of multiple occupancy. At the top of the road, you turn right at the handsome St Peter's Church, into Montpelier Road. You are then a stone's throw from the prestigious Catholic school, St Benedict's (formerly for boys only, now mixed): just up the hill is the girls' counterpart, St Augustine's Priory School.

All of which, I thought – on my way to view flat twelve, on a rather beautiful spring day, magnolia just beginning to announce its presence, the lime trees budding – seemed to justify Ealing's reputation as 'Queen of the Suburbs'.

It was 1981, two years into the first Thatcher government, the year that Charles and Diana got married, the summer when John McEnroe was breaking rackets at Wimbledon, where he went on to defeat Bjorn Borg in the final of the men's singles, and the last time the UK won Eurovision, with Bucks Fizz. It was the first year that we had ever heard the word 'internet'; Ronald Reagan became President of the United States; and protesters began to picket US bases at Greenham Common.

It was also still the era of the Greater London Council which – before its abolition by Margaret Thatcher five years later – was generous in supporting single women with advantageous mortgages for house purchase. This was how a youngish woman with no family money and only an average income as a junior college lecturer was able to afford to buy a flat. As my contemporaries now acknowledge, we were the lucky generation. We feel both guilty and angry on behalf of our children, nieces, nephews and younger friends, for whom membership of the 'property owning democracy' – a significant ideological plank of Thatcherism – is now a distant dream.

In fact, I knew the block of flats. My friend Tom Moynihan, who worked with me at Ealing Technical College, lived at number nine, just along the corridor from number twelve. Not wanting to invade his privacy on that particular morning, I said I'd drop by briefly. Tom said, 'No, come lengthily.' I guess I did – Tom has long since left, but my stay at number twelve has been lengthy indeed.

Part One

THE ANTHROPOLOGIST

In the corridors and halls of the building I lived in you
could meet, as in a street or market, every sort of person.
The Memoirs of a Survivor (Doris Lessing, 1974)

March 2020

Thirty-nine years since I arrived here, and an unforeseen and unprecedented event has changed the landscape, both at The Orchard and further afield. A time for reflection, reassessment, a realignment of identity – a shift from 'resident' to 'observer', even anthropologist as, with more than usual scrutiny, I contemplate the people with whom I will be sharing a new way of life over weeks, maybe months. Possibly longer. No one is sure.

Lockdown

'Yeah! Whoah. Oh, yes, yes! Yes, yes, yes!

'One two three four, two left two right, come on, keep upright.

'Two more – come on. One two, kick, kick. There you go. That's better. Niiice!

'Hold it! Have a rest!'

I realise that at seven o'clock in the evening my next-

3

door neighbour Bart must be leading his daily workouts, which he shares through Zoom with the whole of The Orchard. It is 25 March 2020 and, as my personal lockdown began earlier than the official date of 23 March, week two of lockdown.

Only a few weeks earlier, I was still walking to the Lane, as we call it. Pitshanger Lane is not a lane at all these days but a suburban high street with aspirations to charm and neighbourliness. On that Friday I bumped into Carl, secretary of Hanger Hill ward Labour Party, with his labradoodle. Sylvia from Questors, the local theatre club, still planning her cruise of the Baltic. Fred, who used to work with me at UCL, was queuing in the popular, always busy greengrocers, Charlie's Fruit Bowl. We were defiant then. Just the week before, Alice in the book group was saying that the Covid hysteria was 'a fuss about nothing'. I had agreed. There is a queue at the butchers today – the first distancing experience. But the fishmonger is oddly empty. Perhaps people don't eat fish in a crisis, rather comfort food like pies or scones or jelly and custard. The camp young fishmonger, always cute in his neat wellies, tosses in an extra piece of fish for me. He's taken to doing this lately.

People behaving badly, I note, as thousands head off to Richmond Park over the first weekend of lockdown or much further afield to Snowdonia. This rush is, my friend Romy and I concur, the triumph of individualism over the collective. The reasoning is: I'm just one family and we are going to a wild, uninhabited place where we won't disturb anyone. It's just me. Fine, unless about ten thousand other people have exactly the same idea. Which they do.

During the second week of my personal lockdown, on 24 March, I write in my diary, 'the news is terrible.

The greatest number of deaths in one day, eighty-seven, with twenty-two of them at Northwick Park Hospital'. Northwick Park is one of our local hospitals which has reported 'a crisis'. We are nervous. Yes, this is leafy suburbia and all that, but the pandemic is close to home. We are privileged yet vulnerable. Early on, a commentator notes: 'we were aware that if a coronavirus wave was destined for the capital, the boroughs served by Northwick Park – Harrow, Brent and Ealing – would be likely to be hit hard'.

A few weeks later, a daily death rate of eighty-seven will be something to be celebrated.

On 25 March, I write in my diary: 'if and when we get through this, so much will have changed – friendships, social relationships, wider society. The landscape will look different'. This is hardly a novel thought: many left-wing commentators of a more optimistic turn claim that Covid will signal an end to the marketisation of everything, that the need for cooperation and solidarity will prevail over a dominant individualistic culture. Others think that the outcome will be a surge in support for the right, a return to nationalism, a drawing down, a looking inwards, rather than an opening outwards. In the first week, we talk politics endlessly over the phone. 'I like to think that this terrible business might mark a sea change when the madness of Brexit and the sheer nastiness of Johnson and Cummings will be seen for what it is. We are now forced to listen to the despised "experts" who are prepared to acknowledge what they don't know'. All this in another entry in the diary, during that first week.

At the end of the week my diary reads: 'Jennifer, as mad as ever, suggests we go out with fans'. This is the time when a lot of batty ideas are doing the rounds. Massive amounts of vitamin C or D is another one. And my friend Una suggests gargling with TCP. I even try that, for about a day.

By week two, a routine is established. I stagger down the stairs to the entrance hall to collect *The Guardian*, delivery of which has proved complicated. Sometimes it's stolen, probably by a passing jogger, and I am irrationally annoyed by this. You get petty in lockdown. My dear friend Edward, now with dementia, offers a rare joke: 'Well at least they are intellectual thieves,' he says as consolation during my regular phone calls to him. I pass a young couple in the hallway. I imagine they see a batty old crone, hair awry, tatty dressing gown. When they ask, 'who are you?', I'm tempted to say, 'I'm the anthropologist', recalling the slightly laboured joke about the research done on the Navajo Nation by white scholars in the United States. They would move into their 'research sites' for years. When asked about their family units, the native people would say, 'Well there are five of us in this house, two adults, two kids and the anthropologist.'

'I'm the anthropologist – documenting lockdown in The Orchard,' I could say to the new couple from flat nine, but I don't.

The Old-Timers and the New Cosmopolitans

Early in the outbreak of the virus pandemic, people started talking about the great British spirit during the war. The Blitz. Churchill. How we 'all stood together' and 'wasn't the Queen Mother wonderful' sort of thing. I'm an Old-Timer. I was born during the war, but I don't remember the royals being wonderful. My mother loathed the Queen Mother to her dying day. My memories are patchy and random, like you couldn't get bananas; sweets were rationed; and we had meals considered strange now, like tripe and onions, or frugal suppers, such as a single egg poached in a Pyrex dish, with lots of bread and butter to fill up with. As for the drama of actual war, I'm sure I saw a gas mask one time in the cupboard under the stairs, which all houses had then. What happened to those cupboards under the stairs?

Now that we don't go out, beyond the allowed one period of daily exercise, it seems important to know who I am sharing lockdown with in this part of West London. One day, with not much to do – there are many such days now – I tick off the neighbours. Six flats on each floor going clockwise. It is an unusual numbering system. We begin with flat three and end with flat twenty. No one has ever come up with an explanation for this.

Flat three: the Italians – Luca, Valentina and their son Lorenzo. Luca is a baker in Richmond, now on furlough. Furlough. All the new words we never used before. 'What is "furlough" in Italian?' I ask Luca, but don't remember the answer.

Flat four: empty. Juan, originally from Cape Verde, has moved out, to the relief of Anna and Armando next door. Juan was fun and chatty when you met him, but there was unexplained crashing and yelling, often at three o'clock in the morning. He tried to sell me Moroccan tiles for my new kitchen. Juan's move away was a bit of a midnight flit, so no goodbyes there.

Flat five: Anna and Armando, who have been there forever. Great couple, charming, low-key, but always ready with the offer of a glass of wine on a Friday night. Armando has already set me up with an iPad, formerly resisted but a useful Covid companion.

Flat six: for several years, it was the two primary schoolteachers, Jenny and Patty. I came to call them the Wild Girls, following a memorable moving-in do, the harbinger of a succession of frenzied parties. They moved on, as did Becky and Leonard and their sons who replaced them. Very recently, just a few weeks in advance of Covid, Hungarians – Eszter and Tamás and their boys, Gergő and Balint – arrived.

Flat seven: Hanna, of Polish heritage, with – I think – a new boyfriend, unless Ziggy has done something strange to his hair in lockdown.

Flat eight: Joe, a painter, went to art school in Australia but does painting and decorating as well as his work on giant canvases, glimpsed through the windows of his ground-floor flat. Rarely seen, though great to talk to when you pin him down.

Flat nine: new, young couple.

Flat ten: Jannis, an archivist at one of London's universities. Though a long-time Orchard resident and very polite and pleasant when you run into her, she never socialises.

Flat eleven: Bart and Emma, fairly new arrivals from Australia. Bart is Vietnamese but was adopted, as a baby, by an Australian family. He's a children's writer and actor, as well as taking on stunt work in films and TV. He is also a fitness instructor and into something called Pogo Pulse. His partner Emma works for an international pharmaceutical company. The love of their lives is their Hungarian pointer, Darius.

Flat twelve: me.

Flat thirteen: James and Simone, newly married. James is the director of a charity called The Book Bus, which supports literacy in the UK and in developing countries, working much of the time in Zambia where he met Simone. The Book Bus sports original designs, done free of charge by the illustrator Quentin Blake.

Flat fourteen: Emil, a striking man, of confident bearing, often mistaken for the arts correspondent for the BBC, to whom he bears a strong resemblance. Parents Polish but brought up in Britain. He worked for a time as Director of Finance for Thames Water – a company of spectacular incompetence. This has led to teasing by his Orchard friends. Through Emil's window on the first floor, you can see a display of hats, and once I saw a red ballet shoe perched on top of a pile of books.

I move mentally to the top floor.

Flat fifteen: I think this is Stephanie and Rob. Very sweet couple.

Flat sixteen: this must be Joanna. I cannot place her, but she is a star at the daily Zoom workout sessions, says Bart.

Flat seventeen: good friends here: Harold and Eileen. They are now in Norfolk. In fairness, not part of the group who left their London homes to 'escape' to the country, as Norfolk has been their main home for some time.

Flat eighteen: Basabdatta, Anirban and their little boy Arin, originally from India. The couple are very successful in IT. They seem to have devised some strenuous exercise to keep fit during lockdown. There is a thundering noise for about twenty minutes every day at four o'clock. It no longer bothers me. They are a delightful family. I haven't seen them for weeks. Not even a glimpse on the back stairs.

Flat nineteen: Irene, from Russia, replaced Peter the Slovakian, a cultured but troubled man, always in a great coat and trilby, which he tipped in old European style to passing women. Peter disappeared suddenly one day. No one was sure if this was due to personal or money difficulties. Now Irene has also moved on – with her bloke, to Watford – to be replaced by a beautiful young Indian couple who seem friendly enough when I meet them going out for the daily jog – theirs not mine.

Flat twenty: Chikayo teaches at the Japanese School in Ealing. Much liked by her Orchard neighbours, partly because she brings wonderful fresh sushi to The Orchard Christmas parties. She regularly reverses into the electricity metres at the back of the flats.

A few weeks into lockdown, Chikayo sends an email, Haiku-like, in answer to our offer of help in lockdown:

Thank you for your letter
I appreciate your help
I feel I'm not alone
Take care

It comes as a shock to realise that I am by far the oldest resident, both in biological and Orchard years. The relatively recent newcomers, whom I call the New Cosmopolitans, are younger, ethnically diverse, tending to come from every corner of the globe. A few years ago, though I hardly thought about it at the time, British-born residents became a minority at The Orchard. The Old-Timers, as I came to call them, are: me, James, Joe, Emil and Harold and Eileen in flat seventeen.

We Old-Timers are white and sort of British. I say 'sort of' as Emil is of Polish heritage; Joe, raised in Greater Manchester, spent many years as a young adult in Australia; and James is Northern Irish – still British, but now we have Brexited, who knows what lies down that particular road? I have just acquired an Irish passport, on the basis of my father's birthplace, so I'm Irish too. Two passports and nowhere to go.

Angels

Simone and James have offered to do shopping for me. We shout along the corridor, as they return from the supermarket in full lockdown gear, as if prepared for a nuclear strike:

Cathie: 'Was it hell?'

James: 'No, it was heaven. Full of angels.'

Cathie: 'You're my angels.'

In gratitude, I make some soggy banana bread – more like a very chewy biscuit – and place it neatly outside James and Simone's door. Simone emails to say that 'interesting flavours are coming through', possibly the cumin seeds and curry powder I threw in to give it a bit of a kick. I don't much like bananas – or avocados – an ungrateful thought when Anna and Armando leave industrial quantities of both outside my back door. I know Emil will be an avocado man, so I leave them outside number fourteen. It's like the old Soviet days – a total absence of flour but a surplus of bananas. A few days later, there is a meal for me, displayed in front of number twelve on a little table, doily and a small pot of spices to add to the fried chicken. So elegantly served. Simone's handiwork, I realise. We contemplate setting up a local barter economy. I can trade you bananas for eggs; toilet paper for bleach. This was before Trump proposed it as an antidote for the virus and some poor chap in Maryland swallowed a whole bottle.

Emil is another angel. He brings goodies from Morrisons, basics but some delicious Stilton too, feeling embarrassed about the mousetrap he brought last time. Another time, Luca brings a seeded loaf from his bakery. We talk at a distance on the lawn – well, if you can call it a lawn. It's not a lawn in the usually understood sense, more a stretch of grass. Emil likes talking politics, so there's a fair bit of ranting. It seems he knew Tony Benn. I make a note to myself to talk to him about this when we are back to having proper conversations. Emil is good on Priti Patel stories. Admittedly there are a fair few of these around. After one of Patel's rare – I wonder why? – public appearances, Emil says that she makes Diane Abbott look like Sir Isaac Newton. I bridle – I like Diane Abbott – but have to agree about the Tory Home Secretary. Patel has just boasted that crime has come down under her watch, especially shoplifting, prompting from Emil, 'Doesn't she realise that the shops are all closed?!' This said as he rushes off – Emil always has to be somewhere in a hurry – adding the parting shot that it's time for 'Hancock's Half Hour', the daily government briefing led by Matt Hancock, the Secretary of State for Health.

It's only weeks ago, though it seems years, since I bumped into Emil at the opera, feeling slightly self-conscious as we champagne socialists do, when caught among the haute bourgeoisie. That evening there's a new ballet and the place is stuffed with luvvies. My actor friend introduces me to several TV celebrities who look as glossy and glamorous as on the screen. I've worn my best frock but still feel shabby. I've never seen so many rich and thin women, impossibly thin and probably impossibly rich too, as indicated by the presence of a genuine fur coat, almost never seen in London these days. Its owner has to wear it in the auditorium, I imagine, as she wouldn't dare leave it in the cloakroom, not even at Covent Garden. She looks at her smartphone most of the evening.

All of this is now a thing of the past, and though the poor have been much more affected by the virus than the wealthy, 'the garden', as they call it, will be closed, along with the local football club. The last time I was on a bus was with a crowd from Brentford. At that point in early March, the pandemic was just on the horizon. I had caught the 65 bus to Kew Gardens to meet my friend Sagal, who was dying to see the orchids, until I realised that Brentford were playing at home that day. On the way back to Ealing Broadway, the bus was heaving.

Joe is getting a food parcel delivered – he says because he is in the one and a half million of particularly vulnerable people who've received the famed NHS letter, warning them to be especially careful in Covid times. Joe looks healthy. However, he tells me that he has bad asthma and ulcerative colitis. 'They send only loads of spuds, carrots and tins of tomato soup,' he says. 'You wouldn't want to eat that.'

'So what *do* you eat?' I ask.

'I slip off to Marks and Spencer first thing in the morning,' he says. Joe leaves a supply of tomato soup, baked beans and carrots outside my door the next morning.

The Clapping

Towards the end of week two, new routines are falling into place. One is the clapping. On the first Thursday – it's always Thursday – I do a feeble lone clap out of the window. Where is everybody else? By the following week, things have perked up a bit and Emil promises to look out of his first-floor window at number fourteen, while I stand below on the concourse: 'Romeo and Juliet in reverse', as he says. And so, each week at eight o'clock, I stand at the front of The Orchard. At first it is odd but nice to spot Joe, lurking behind his curtain in his ground-floor flat. Then Chikayo appears at her upper-floor window, before Emil finally makes a showing at the window of flat fourteen. Something that seems a bit tacky sort of works. Hidden behind blinds and curtains, there is the joy of human company, of the human voice, as we shout to each other.

'How are you?'

'Are you OK?'

Chikayo nods and smiles.

'Joe, are you getting any painting done?'

Joe points to a huge canvas just visible on the wall behind him. James and Simone, absorbed in domesticity and serious cooking, rarely emerge. However, a few weeks later, James appears, banging a saucepan and – drawing on his Ulster roots – proclaims that he's 'practising for the marching season'. Only Emil and I understand the cultural reference to the Apprentice Boys march in Derry, celebrating the Battle of the Boyne.

That Thursday is also the day that Boris Johnson returns, after five weeks away ill with the virus, to front the briefing sessions. He is now a father again, for the sixth or seventh time – no one is too sure. I note in my diary, 'fortunately there is not too much smirking and simpering over the child, Wilfred'.

A few weeks later and the weekly clap has the feel of a duty. The early flurry of sociability and spontaneity has subsided. That first evening now seems an age ago, and there is something tawdry about this celebratory moment, when so many of the health workers and other public servants on the front line, such as bus drivers, have died for lack of proper equipment and protection.

The time for clapping is over.

THE WORLD GETS SMALLER

The strict rules mean citizens are only permitted to leave their houses to shop for basic necessities, for medical reasons, to travel to/from work when absolutely necessary – and for one form of exercise a day.

Government guidelines, April 2020

May 2020

Now May and outside the world is glorious: nature is enjoying our absence – the foxes, the blue tits taking charge, a pair of jays – I didn't even know jays did pairs; I thought they were solitary, like robins, though I also saw two robins together, unusually sociable. As we isolate, they bond. It isn't so much that new birds or creatures appear, as that they are more confident in their demeanour. The foxes look healthy, glossy-coated, magnificent even. Their stride is majestic, their gaze direct, defiant; no more skulking, nipping through holes in the fence at dusk. The squirrels are dramatically acrobatic. The blackbird I see as I stand outside The Orchard in early morning has its beak fully stuffed with twigs on its way to a nest.

We are settling into lockdown. With life curtailed and confined, the world gets smaller but comes more sharply into focus. Very early one morning, a graceful young woman does yoga in the garden. Moving into an elegant headstand, she is barely recognisable, but it is Hanna from flat seven, looking different in yoga kit. Luca and Valentina sit to have a smoke on Kim's seat. Bart and Emma do impressively athletic exercises on the grass out the back, watched by their handsome dog, Darius. Dogs are not really allowed – we all have memories of the yapping little horrors that belonged to Elena at number eighteen, some years ago now – but the dog is a beauty and well behaved, so we have given Bart, Emma and Darius the benefit of the doubt.

The Fox and the Rat

The two Hungarian boys from flat six below me rush around the lawn once released from home tuition, which their mum takes very seriously. Before they are set free to play, I hear the phonics practice, drifting up to my window. B – o – a – t. Simone finds a spot just by the garage to scroll through her emails, as James does manly stuff with motorbikes and his old Volvo. The days have a new rhythm and a predictability. The same robin appears each morning, a single fox at dusk. At least Luca and I decide that it is the same one – 'he or she', as he says. Luca is very conscious of gender, making much of this crucial grammatical difference between English and Italian, during our ad hoc Italian lessons, as we chat out the front of the building. I decide it's a vixen, as I spot her late at night with a cub – well, either that or a large rat. Maybe the basis for a children's story? *The Fox and the Rat*. Anna also sees the cunning little vixen, as I now call her, when she goes out very early for her jog.

The vixen at The Orchard

North or south

Many of us have our key texts as a point of reference in lockdown. *La Peste* is an obvious one, along with Daniel Defoe's *A Journal of the Plague Year*. Mine is *The Memoirs of a Survivor* by Doris Lessing. In Lessing's novel, an unnamed threat leads people to abandon the city, as happened in London, when at the outbreak of the virus, folk headed for the second home in Devon or Sussex. Ripe pickings for burglars, I reflect spitefully, with all those posh flats in Kensington standing empty.

BL (Before Lockdown), I used to head south to the Lane or east to the Broadway. Often, from there, into town. Now the parameters of my life have shrunk. 'Exercise only close to home', we've been told. I'm surprised at my compliance, but for weeks now, it has been left out of The Orchard and up the hill or, on alternate days, a matter of a few steps right to the

Arboretum, a fancy name for the small park which is next to Montpelier Primary School.

Left and up the hill takes me to Hanger Hill Park, Fox Lane and the adjacent woods where steeply raked steps lead up to the football pitches, the only hazard here being the joggers 'flattening old ladies in the park'. I bump into neighbours or acquaintances: Pete from the Labour Party. 'What do you think of Starmer?' we yell at each other from different sides of the street. I love Pete, but now, in enforced isolation, even people I don't usually care for much become attractive.

'How are you doing?'

'How's the homeschooling going?' we shout across the two metres. Shared humanity trumps petty antipathies.

One day, quite early on when spring is still a novelty, I have a delightful walk through Fox Woods. A woman of about my age stops, as we do the now-customary dance to shimmy past each other on the narrow path. As often, these are moments for a chat – as we distance physically, mitigation seems in order. We admire the green of the trees. What I had always thought a slightly tatty piece of woodland is now magical, *Hansel and Gretel*, a place of wonder you might get lost in. The woman in Fox Woods says that she writes poetry. So many people do. I remember a chance encounter with another woman – Sandra – on the train to Swansea. Rather good too, I realised, when she sent me some verses in the post. But the useful thing about my new acquaintance is that she can do Zoom. I have recently acquired an iPad, said to be an essential tool for lockdown, especially Zoom. Joan – that's her name – says she's been forced into it in order to contact grandchildren.

'Just press "accept" on the screen,' she says. I go home and the job is done.

If I turn right down Montpelier Road, I come to the Arboretum. The casual visitor would not realise what it is. There are exotic-looking trees, mostly without labels, as the council can't afford a full-time arborist. But a park ranger tells me one day that the Caucasian wingnut is quite rare. It is true what everyone says – you really do look at things more closely, as day-to-day life closes in. I now pay very particular attention to the wingnut. I notice also that a magnolia tree has encircled a young lime tree, and a root of an ancient cypress has somehow wound its way back around the tree so that it gently cradles part of the trunk, like a hand. I decide to take photographs of their embrace.

All of this makes me think of Joe, our resident artist at The Orchard – though he'd hate that term. Before lockdown, I would meet him down the Broadway – he was drawing trees in Pitshanger Park at that time. I told him to look out for the Caucasian wingnut in the Arboretum. Also, how the ranger had said – I don't know how it came up – that trees are immortal. I've been trying to work that out. Lockdown makes philosophers of us all. I am inspired by the beauty of the wingnut, whether immortal or not, and, during my ambulation round the park, learn the names of its comrades: the Caucasian elm, the handkerchief tree – no label there but I know that one anyway – black poplar, lime trees, cypress, the Turkish oak, south-western sweet gum, sequoias or the redwoods of California. Represented are Turkey, Russia, the American Southwest, China. One particular lime tree is spectacular, though the ranger has said that it may eventually collapse under the weight of its many branches. The lime is magnificent, but the handkerchief tree is my favourite. It has other names, all beautiful, whether they are the Latin or popular names. I read later on Wikipedia:

> *Davidia involucrata, the dove-tree, handkerchief tree, pocket handkerchief tree, or ghost tree, is a medium-sized deciduous tree in the family Nyssaceae. It was previously included with tupelos in the dogwood family, Cornaceae. It is native to South Central and Southwest China from Hubei to southern Gansu, south to Guizhou, Sichuan.*

About six weeks into lockdown, I bump into Joe round the back of the flats, near the bins, just where Chikayo always reverses into the electricity meters. Joe is still drawing trees, but he isn't interested in documenting or prettifying, or, like me, taking photographs I consider aesthetically pleasing. He is drawing just one tree, not a fancy one in the actual Arboretum, but just on the edge. He is interested in the way it is shaped at the top. He tells me that he wants to walk out of his studio – one room in his small flat – feeling he has done something different. Joe, not interested in selling his work – he's a process artist – insists that it must be the work *itself* which has poetry. 'A four-year-old child can do something wonderful,' he says.

Seeking the light

Fifty days. At first the phone went constantly. Now it is silent. At the same time, Orchard life is taking on a new kind of rhythm. It all seems the same, and yet nothing is the same. The heavy-duty gardeners still turn up and are here today. They don't garden in the normally understood sense, but flatten and clear out, vigorously and noisily.

The result is tidy but spartan and oddly chilling. Karol and Boris, big Polish guys, demolish everything in their path. Emil calls it the Chernobyl effect. Laurie, the gentle gardener, comes the other days. There is rivalry. We have to keep them apart. Now, in week seven, people are beginning cautiously to appear outside, like plants who've long been in the dark, seedlings in need of warmth and sunlight.

Seedling. I'm reminded of my friend Andrew, who lives just down the road, in Shepherd's Bush. In the early lockdown days, he was kept awake by his beloved cat. The cat was poorly. Did he sense that things were different? Now that the cat has died, Andrew's nurturing self is drawn to gardening for the first time, and he is kept awake by new thoughts such as, *I didn't water the seedlings.* At The Orchard, I see – is it Riccardo or Luca? – with a little boy, who I realise must be Lorenzo, make a rare foray into the garden with a jar of water. It seems the boy has planted two seedlings which he needs to water. Just across the road from The Orchard, someone has created two tiny plots. Looking closer than I normally would, I see that they are vegetable gardens, mere patches of earth but growing marrows and beans. Andrew's partner Tonny, who is a carer – admittedly for rather well-off people in Chelsea – has moved into their homes to look after them; my friend Una is sewing scrubs for the workers in her local psychiatric hospital; Simone makes glorious cakes, mountains of chocolate and butter icing. One, left outside my door sometime in April, is a version of an Easter cake, I realise. Whatever happened to Easter?

I talk from my window. There's a lot of that now, as The Orchard takes on some of the feel of a Spanish barrio. I call to Anna and Armando drinking white wine in the garden. They say, 'come on down', but I feel grotty and have just run a bath. So we shout at a distance. We are too British to sing opera from our windows – as they have taken to doing in some parts of Italy during the Covid restraints – but we agree that a gentle drink is in order – if the weather improves by the weekend.

It is surreal to talk to people on the phone or email when they are a stone's throw away. When we do catch sight of each other, we peer at each other like strange ghostly creatures from another planet. We are shy.

The days are acquiring a pattern in glorious spring. I go into the garden quite early – I decide to start having breakfast, at least coffee, at that little green iron table, the one my friend Ruth Marks had all those years ago on the balcony in her flat in Maida Vale. Around lunchtime, the Hungarian family may opt for a makeshift picnic, just below their windows in their ground-floor flat. Their two boys, Gergő and Balint, play in the late-ish afternoon, before Armando and Anna have a glass of wine before dinner. Earlier than that, Luca and Valentina may have a smoke or, if it's warm, Joe sits on the bench, the old green one that gets the sun at a particular time of the afternoon. He wears a Van Gogh-like straw hat and reads, but only for an hour or so. Joe is a rare bird, who appears seldom and only ever settles in one place. For Joe it is the old green bench, not the newer posh Lutyens seat that we got in memory of our handyman Kim. Emil never sits in the garden.

I say that, but even Emil seeks the sun. One day there he is, sitting on Kim's bench with an attractive blonde, drinking Prosecco and settling into a substantial lunch. They are definitely not social distancing.

In this together or just me

It's week eight by my tally. At The Orchard, we are distant yet closer. People's lives are on display outside their doors; Emil has put an elegant bag on his doormat – what do you call those bags, leather and expensive, old-fashioned, what used to be doctors' bags? A Gladstone bag, that's it. This one has an elegant little key attached. Cooking – which people are doing more of – smells enticing, exotic. James says that he and Simone are going African-style this week, goat stew. Their shoes sit neatly side by side outside their door; they never were before. As lives are more fully lived in smallish flats, they spill over into the long, shared corridor of our thirties-era block of flats. From another flat – maybe the new couple? – Bach drifts along the corridor like the smells of Simone's cooking.

Things are much harder for families not a stone's throw from here, in the poorer part of the borough. Sarah, the headteacher of one of the most disadvantaged schools in Ealing, talks of children going hungry in families where school lunch is the meal of the day for the kids. Lured back into school, despite fears of the virus, where poor children are provided for even in lockdown, one little boy had three dinners, one after the other, Sarah tells me.

Poverty and privilege. It is week nine, Saturday, 23 May, and the story of the day is Dominic Cummings' dash out of the city at the height of the epidemic to his parents' farm in Durham. As his wife's family own a castle, one imagines they were rather spoilt for choice. 'Well, darling, is it the castle or Mummy and Daddy's farm?' What apparently was not possible was to stay in their London home, like everyone else. And have the whole family got bladders of concrete that they do not need a pit stop on the way from Islington to Durham? Will he be able to brazen this through? That's the question of the hour. He does.

Again, the triumph of individualism over the collective. Cummings boasts, along with the Tory stooges, including the supposedly politically neutral Attorney General Suella Braverman, about how wonderful it is to put your wife and child first. Don't they realise that the whole point of a collective struggle – which fighting a virus has to be – is that you *don't* put your own first? But their philosophy is simple: it's just *me* – or *mine, my* wife, *my* child, *my* property – and these are the people who dare to talk about *my* country. Of course they are right. It is their country, forged in their name, its institutions designed to serve their interests.

Garden stories

I learn new things. As I practise my Italian with Luca in the garden, it turns out flat three is not Luca, Valentina and their little boy, but a sort of ménage à trois as Riccardo – who I thought was just a strange hanger-on – is Lorenzo's father. When lockdown struck, Riccardo had lost his job as a cook in a local Italian restaurant and had nowhere to go. So he moved into flat three. I have only seen the boy when he came out to water his seedlings, and Luca tells me that the child – or 'the kid' as he calls him, is terribly lazy and a bit of a baby – didn't I hear him screeching when Riccardo tried to cut his hair? Hair is a problem all round of course, with all the barbers closed: some have put bandanas round their hair; Joe's has grown shoulder-length. Simone has a short Afro, usually very elegantly scarved. James cuts her hair, she tells me. She must do his, as it looks quite stylish.

I talk to Luca, who wanders up to chat in the garden one day, and we have that old debate about how you make spaghetti carbonara. Pretentiously, I consider it my signature dish. Clearly this cuts no ice with Luca, who insists on cream, *guancia* of pork and pecorino. I knew about the pecorino – parmesan is a very poor substitute – OK I knew that, but surely not cream, and surely the meat needs to be pancetta rather than cheek of pork? My Italian is patchy, little grammar apart from the subjunctive and lots of vocabulary, so I know that *guancia* is 'cheek'.

Around week ten, four of us decide daringly to break the rules and have drinks in the garden. Two bottles – one white, one red – are placed in the centre of the grass. Luca has brought a brew of his own.

Luca tells us he worked at Subway when he first came to Britain, then – before ending up at the high-end bakers, Gails – was at Wetherspoons, which he loved. Anna, Armando and I are dismayed, as Tim Martin, who owns Wetherspoons, is a mad Brexiteer. We all lament the dismal performance of the Tory government, with Luca exclaiming that Johnson is just like Berlusconi! Not an original thought perhaps, but we all nod. No reference is made to the fact that it is actually VE Day and more conventionally patriotic people are at that moment having their street parties, in defiance of lockdown.

A few months ago – even over Christmas – we might have talked about Brexit, due then to be finalised at the end of January. Now Brexit seems not just an eternity away, but entirely irrelevant, along with the dramatis personae of that particular drama. Rees-Mogg – whatever happened to him? Well, actually, as Armando points out, he's still there, Leader of the House of Commons, God help us.

Nigel Farage has his own radio show. On this particular spring evening, we share new and old stories about Ealing and The Orchard: how Ho Chi Minh worked as a baker in the hotel round the corner; how in my flat at number twelve lived a famous pop group; how one of us met Kate Middleton as a teenager, now the Princess of Wales, and thought she was a go-getting little minx. This segues neatly and inevitably into the story of Kate's mum, Carole Middleton, who went to a comprehensive school just along the Uxbridge Road, down in Southall. A successful school, it is attended – because of the demography of the surrounding community – largely by pupils of Indian origin. When I told the story of Carole Middleton to a local teacher, himself Indian, Sameer – not missing a beat – replied:

I didn't know Kate's mum was Indian.

We've heard the stories – and the jokes – many times before, but there is comfort in the retelling. Once again, I tell the story about being on a tour in Vietnam, how when the tour guide told the story about Ho Chi Minh and Ealing – feeling like a schoolgirl who can please sir with a good answer – my hand had shot up. 'I come from Ealing.' When he added, 'the name of the hotel was Drayton Manor Hotel', my hand shot up again. 'Still there,' I shriek, 'just round the corner. We have our Labour Party ward meetings there.'

The end of Eden

It is the start of week eleven. Our lockdown Eden is beginning to fray round the edges. I hear Riccardo and

Luca shouting outside, round the back of the garages. Could it be that the hitherto comfortable ménage is under stress? This is hardly surprising, as Luca explains: 'It is strange. We did it [moved into flat three together] because it was not possible to sort it out with the kid and it was going to be really expensive to find a flat just for two people. So we organised to help each other... so we found The Orchard. Obviously, they [Riccardo and Valentina] broke up a long time ago – long time ago – so it's not like a weird situation that one of the two is still in love with the other. We are friends. We help each other... with the kid and er other things. Obviously, it's not the best situation in the world, but we are foreign people in the country. That's especially now after Covid and Brexit. The situation is not getting any better, to be honest.'

At The Orchard, harmony and goodwill are breaking down. Emil has noticed cigarette butts over the grass, even a fag put out on the seat we had made for our much-loved handyman Kim. 'This isn't downtown Naples,' he mutters – though Luca is from Genoa and Riccardo from Sardinia, I point out gently.

And I thought we were a multicultural hub.

Luca is full of apologies. '*Scussami tanto. Mi dispiace multisimmo. Non faccio piu, ti prometto.*' He leaves a seeded loaf outside Emil's door, as a peace offering.

But then there are the bees. They have burrowed into the mortar. I think at first they are masonry bees, but the pest control guy from the council says they are regular bumblebees who appear to have found a comfy home in the gap in the outside wall. Valentina is distraught. She has a phobia, can't sleep a wink, as the bees are right there in the wall by her bed. She insists that the gardeners –

probably Karol and Boris for this job – chop down all the flowering bushes to get rid of the bees. I try to explain that bees are part of nature, the life cycle, not vermin to be destroyed. Valentina is not persuaded.

And the adorable vixen has a darker side. Anna thinks it is more horror story than child's fable – of course the two have much in common. As we gossip in the garden, Anna says how one evening she was taken aback by the vixen's stare of hostility. 'Look, you suckers, we're in charge now,' the animal seemed to say. This view is clinched by Hanna. When I ask why she has taken down the feeders, really meant for birds but used by Hanna to watch the squirrels from her window on the ground floor, she says she saw a fox 'right there' – she points to the spot. 'And – there's no nice way to say this – the fox ate the squirrel right there in front of me.'

Forbidden territory

For weeks now, the Broadway has been off-limits, forbidden territory. Strange when that stretch of road has been part of my life for so many years. Will today be the day I go forth into those streets? Another text comes to mind. *The Road* by Cormac McCarthy, the apocalyptic story of a nuclear disaster, where everything has been laid waste.

I finally walk that further block down to the Broadway. Joe, who has ventured further than me in recent weeks on his way to Marks and Spencer, had said that it is back to normal. But it isn't. While human life has stalled Mary Celeste-style, nature has moved on. The chestnut blossoms have gone. Oaks and other trees I barely noticed before are in full leaf. Haven Green itself, whose flower beds are usually kept in some kind of shape, has been abandoned, the grass knee-high. All the cafes that face the green are closed. It looks sad. 'Neglected' is the word that comes to mind. The buses, normally full of school kids, shoppers, old people who love to flaunt their freedom passes, are still almost empty. And, of course, there are the masks.

The Broadway was never pretty, but it had a vitality. Now people hang out aimlessly, with nowhere to go. At one time, the green would have been full of people lingering on their way to eat out or go to a pub. Gone is the sense of purposefulness – the soul, as James suggests. I never thought of Ealing as having 'soul'. But I know what he means.

Another day. The daily death toll reaches over forty thousand. Early on, I see the young vixen and a jay in the sycamore tree outside my window. Hanna is meditating on her yoga mat. Armando leaves more sourdough outside my back door. People are talking of getting together, even barbecues. Emil is keen.

I hear an ice-cream van and then young Balint in flat six downstairs shouting, 'Ice-cream bell!' A sound from Before Lockdown. Haunting, unearthly.

ARRIVAL AT THE ORCHARD

I am moving in
Next door to you
So you can get to know me,
You will see my shadow
In the bathroom window,
My aromas will occupy
Your space,
Our ball will be in your court.
How will you feel?

From 'Neighbours' by Benjamin Zephaniah

June 1981

The small crowd gathered that night at The Orchard were comfortably pleased with themselves. It was two years since the surprise election of Margaret Thatcher, Britain's first woman prime minister, and a year away from the Falklands War, which helped to extend her reign till 1990. Across London, it was a time of turbulence. In April, Brixton in South London had witnessed violent clashes between the black community and the Metropolitan police. Closer to home and still scarred in local memory was the death, two years earlier in April 1979, of Blair

Peach. Blair Peach, a New Zealand teacher, was hit on the head during an Anti-Nazi League Demonstration in Southall, probably by a member of the Special Patrol Group, a specialist unit within the Metropolitan Police Service. He died in hospital that night.

But on that particular early summer evening in 1981, these events, significant as they were, did not preoccupy us. This was an occasion for pleasantries, not politics.

The golfer look, which I had affected for a few years – wide-legged trousers, soft blazers – had transitioned into the sharper shoulder pads of the eighties which came to typify the early Thatcher era. I remember opting not for the power suit I sometimes wore to work, but a floaty affair, hippy-ish top and midi skirt, perhaps even those knee-length white boots. All of which, I thought, would endear me to my new neighbours.

A soirée

There were ten people, as I recall. All strangers to me, apart from Jill and Douglas Appleby, whom I had met briefly, as we negotiated the sale of flat twelve. Pleasant, middle class and white: the Applebys – moving to a mock Tudor estate in West Acton – Mavis and Ron and Dack and Holda were all undoubtedly present that evening. Also Gerald Horrocks and his stylish, much younger French wife, Jeanne. Everyone in pairs. Well, not me, and not Tom, who taught English Literature at Ealing, which had now transitioned into Ealing College of Higher Education, though I tended to stick to its old name, Ealing Tech. Such a nice idea, everyone agreed, that Jill and Douglas should offer this newcomer a chance to meet her neighbours. The wine was plonk – Sainsbury's – but lots of it, as well as pineapple and cheese stuck on toothpicks, later sneered at, but then still quite chic. I was reminded of my student parties – we had called them soirées – in the early sixties.

I had first viewed number twelve a few weeks before the evening of the soirée. Of course, I knew the block. Tom lived there. First flat on the left as you went up a short flight of stairs to the second of three floors. But I had never ventured further along a gloomy narrow corridor, at the end of which stood 'my flat', as it came to be, alongside its twin, number eleven.

Twin flats

Severe linoleum, institutional walls and harsh overhead strip lighting, it promised little. And yet, once across the threshold, my impression had been of light, brightness, windows on all sides, overlooking a garden which – though much diminished from its heyday as a proper orchard – still featured a few apple and cherry trees. During that first visit, there was a team of devoted gardeners beavering away. It looked like a first Eden.

Though the block was thirties, the flat – my flat – had been decorated in seventies style. I didn't mind the hideous brown walls, made of cork tiles; I could tolerate even the ugly gas fire. The cork tiles went, though not till around the turn of the century. I see they are suddenly back in vogue, as ecologically friendly. The gas fire remains. I could live with that, I thought. Indeed, I have for the last forty years, along with the art deco-inspired tiles in the bathroom, now cracking and just about clinging to the walls, and the sharp-cornered metal door handles, which regularly puncture your skin. The drama of the replacement windows came later. Only Armando at number five and I stood our ground, refusing to bow to the consensus that PVC was so much more practical. I had wept when confronted with the plastic replacement job which had defaced the original windows in the other sixteen flats, victims of the atrocity.

One story I heard that first night at The Orchard was that a famous pop group had lived right in this flat, the one I was buying, the one we were all drinking and chatting in. The problem was that no one could remember whether it was The Stones, The Animals, The Who, even Queen – all of whom had Ealing connections. Dack was sure it was Keith Richards. Mavis from flat three opted for Pete Townshend. She must have had sight of the interior of the flat because she remembered there was no furniture, just a few large wooden boxes. An old piano had got stuck on the stairs, the front ones, not the out-of-sight back stairs. Eventually, we settled on Fleetwood Mac. This, forty years later, remains the favoured view, though it has never been confirmed.

Douglas, who was a bit of a know-all, claimed knowledge of a host of other Ealing-based pop stars and celebrities. Some stories were in the public domain, for instance that Freddie Mercury had started life in a modest terraced house out west, towards the airport in Heston, before going off to do his art course at the tech. Less well known was that Dusty Springfield had grown up in a smart street round the corner during the 1950s, Kent Gardens, the same street where I'd briefly lived in what the estate agents referred to then as a 'bachelor flat'. I remember my friend Ruth had asked, 'Do they throw the bachelor in with the deal?' Dusty, originally called Mary Isobel Catherine Bernadette O'Brien, attended St Anne's Convent School in Northfields. A handsome plaque has recently appeared there. Before fame and celebrity swept Dusty to the West End, and eventually to Hollywood, she sold gloves at Bentalls department store down the Broadway, which has long since made way for Marks and Spencer.

It was a few years later that Julian Clary, as a scholarship boy, attended St Benedict's, the highly respected independent Catholic school a little further down Montpelier Road, where, so Julian recounted a few years ago:

'between the ages of 11 - 13 I was in the middle school, which was quite a nice, friendly environment. But then you had to go to 'big school' and that was all a bit brutal – it was very macho and all about rugby and cricket.

I was quite a conscientious student and I was well behaved; it didn't occur to me to play truant. I never thought of not turning up or not attending classes, I just endured it every day.

I'm sure the education system is much better today. There was still corporal punishment when I was at St Benedict's, for example, and that's obviously stopped these days. I hear from people who have known the school more recently that it's a lovely, wonderful place now – but in the 70s when I was there, it felt like you were in the 1930s; it was very archaic'. (Julian Clary in *Teach Secondary* 22 September 2015)

Not what they seem

Neither The Orchard nor the Orchardians are quite what they seem. Despite the pretentious canopy over the front door, we have grotty back stairs like a Glasgow tenement. There is the odd fact that we have no street number. Postmen, delivery people and visitors can never find us. There are three floors, with six flats on each floor. An aerial view would show an irregular E shape on each side of the building, with very small flats in the middle of the E, tucked between average-sized flats at the front and more spacious ones at the back, overlooking the garden.

Back stairs at The Orchard

The ground floor

Because the eccentric numbering of the flats means we start with flat three, and as there are eighteen flats, the final flat at the front on the top floor is flat twenty. Of those who were there on the evening of the soirée, Mavis and Ron lived in flat three. Elderly, pleasant enough, no distinguishing features. I am not sure about flat four, though a few years later – long before Juan, the Mexican tiles salesman from Cape Verde, made a lively appearance – was a young woman with an enormous rabbit. I babysat for the rabbit on one occasion. It should be said that this didn't involve anything too onerous, as the rabbit – though not, as I recall, in any kind of hutch – was too fat to move very far. I remember thinking that it was not a very stimulating or attractive kind of a pet. I later learnt that they defecate 350 times a day. What was wrong with a kitten?

At number five was a very elderly lady. The flat had been untouched since the thirties, with all the original features, including a butler's sink. Armando and Anna, much later and with the old sink long since demolished, paid a fortune to install one of the contemporary versions – pretty much identical to its predecessor – in the same flat. Earlier, after the old lady died, and before the long era of Armando and Anna, Jack and Hazel had moved in with their young daughters. Jack and Hazel were the first of a generation which, over the years, replaced a dying population. And the first to introduce children to The Orchard. They were glamorous, bohemian, accomplished painters. Jack taught Turner Prize winner and Oscar-winning film director Steve McQueen at art college – before McQueen achieved an international reputation.

Indeed, Jack had painted a portrait of him. I seem to remember him showing it to me where it was kept in one of the garages out the back. Hazel and Jack, along with their two girls, went off to paint in the South of France. The Orchard seemed shabbier without them.

Nancy, who lived at number six, across the corridor from Hazel and Jack and directly below me, was already quite old when I moved into flat twelve. She was almost completely deaf, and her TV could be heard three blocks away. I went down to complain one day, but Nancy was so charming and apologetic that I was mortified and stayed to chat. It came as no surprise that she had been the Queen's hairdresser. She looked like the person she was, the smile gracious, the silver hair carefully coiffed. She had accompanied the Queen on the famous trip to Kenya when she got the news of her father's death. The details of this once again cannot be verified. Nonetheless, it is now established truth that Nancy was the Queen's hairdresser, just as it is a matter of fact that Fleetwood Mac lived for a time at number twelve.

Nancy's flat and mine were identical in dimensions but couldn't be more different. Hers had a comfy sofa and armchairs, with antimacassars and properly plumped-up cushions. We used to call the sofa – or settee – with the required matching chairs, a 'three-piece suite'. Rather out of fashion now, three-piece suites were then thought to be a central feature of decent bourgeois living rooms. My own furniture was mostly home-made by my dad, who had turned his hand to carpentry in retirement.

I remember that Nancy talked about 'the darkies', now considered a deeply offensive, racist descriptor. Nancy was of that generation who used the term as a matter of course.

I deduce that offence was not intended because, as I recall, what in fact she said, after a stay in Ealing hospital, was, 'the darkies are wonderful to their own families', talking about the food that immigrant families brought in to supplement the meagre hospital rations. As a linguist, I was interested in the effects of the mild stroke that had landed Nancy in hospital. When I went to do shopping for her, once she was no longer able to speak clearly, she wrote down what she wanted. I remember that she spelt Persil: F E R S I N.

Flats seven and eight on the ground floor were unknown territory until much later, when Hanna and Joe respectively took up residence.

The first floor

On my floor at the front, overlooking the street at number nine, was Tom. He stayed for some years until he moved out to live with his girlfriend Jenny. Gary Hoffman, an American who worked at the tech, moved in. Gary was sexy in black leather (Saiorse next door had heard rumours of bondage) and got off with Anna, a cool young Spanish lecturer. Indoor smoking, though not yet illegal, was already frowned upon, and Gary and Anna had bonded over their fags as they huddled outside the Mandela student bar, these days, predictably, renamed Freddie's, in honour of the tech's most famous alumnus, Freddie Mercury. Gary styled himself as a kind of Jack Nicholson character from the *Easy Rider* and *Five Easy Pieces* era. There was a striking resemblance. The gravelly voice, the charm. A kind man, Gary spent hours supporting difficult or struggling students. But as a laid-back Californian, by the time of the harder-nosed mid-eighties, he fell foul of the tough new regime at the then Ealing College of Higher Education. He was brutally and summarily dismissed, on the flimsiest of pretexts – something like poor filing or record keeping. We missed him.

Saoirse at number ten must have arrived at The Orchard sometime after that first soirée. Saoirse O'Brien taught home economics at a local Catholic secondary school and was the aunt of Radiohead lead guitarist Ed O'Brien. Saoirse was beautiful, tragic and Irish. She was highly strung, and I would have to escort her to her front door, two steps along our shared, long corridor, when she had popped round for a glass of wine. 'You never know what might be lurking,' she said. Saoirse had a boyfriend, Oliver, who no one ever saw, leading one to wonder if he actually existed. Whether material or imaginary, Oliver caused her terrible grief. There were many evenings of tears and despair before she eventually left The Orchard, retiring to a bungalow in Somerset.

My nearest neighbours, next door at number eleven, long before my lockdown friends Bart, Emma and Darius had moved in, were pretty much a closed book. A middle-aged woman and her niece. A cat came and went through the cat flap but nothing more eventful. I became friendly with a couple of lawyers, Helena and Nigel, who succeeded the two women and was invited one evening to a very uncomfortable dinner party, the highlight of which was a chocolate fountain. This was the early nineties, and the fountains were a must-have for any kind of social gathering. However – with the fountain malfunctioning and chocolate spurting from every orifice – things went badly wrong. Much like Helena's marriage shortly afterwards. Heartbroken, she moved on. After two unhappy break-ups in flat eleven, a young gay couple, Hal and Jimmy, broke the mould. Their relationship thrived at The Orchard. They wanted to buy and moved to Peckham, a cheaper option than Ealing. Only just as they were leaving, and over a boozy evening together, did I realise what fun they were. Much later, I'm sure I caught a glimpse of Hal doing the Ealing Half Marathon, which now passes right in front of The Orchard each September, waving to me from the bunch of runners.

For a time, there was a single chap, youngish, next door, on the left of the first-floor corridor at number thirteen. I don't recall talking to him at all. And then, suddenly, there was a bailiff's notice pinned to the door. Equally suddenly, the young chap was gone, to be replaced by James.

Next door to James at flat fourteen were Jeanne and Gerald Horrocks. Jeanne, usually called something closer to 'Jan' by her Orchard neighbours – and not her actual name as I was later to discover – was an attractive Parisian. Gerald was slightly built, with neat moustache, sports jacket, cavalry twills, a David Niven kind of a chap, someone you could trust in a crisis. He looked like the assistant headmaster of a preparatory school. Which is what he was. Durston House was known for many years for its 'traditional values' and Christian ethos. Originally a boys' school, it only became co-educational in 2023, long after Gerald's time at the school – 'welcoming girls' as the website graciously puts it. The school is, according to a recent entry in *The Good Schools Guide*, a place where 'traditional Common Entrance subjects are taught with rigour and old-fashioned values, fountain pen and ruler (for underlining, rest assured) at the ready. Male teachers in shirt and tie, addressed as "sir"; the females as "miss"'.

The top floor

On the top floor of The Orchard's three storeys, and moving clockwise from the front of the building at the left as you enter, was Diana at number fifteen, above Tom's flat. She was an accomplished novelist, or had been. Sadly, she was now quite confused and not really able to look after herself. Tom in the flat below testified to unaccounted-for smells, which drifted through the uncovered floorboards. She was devoted to her old mongrel dog. Not an attractive beast. It regularly bit small children.

Apart from Diana, who wandered the local streets looking more and more distrait as the years passed, the only neighbours I recall from the top floor, during the early days, were Dack and Holda in flat eighteen and the elderly gentleman in flat sixteen, living directly above Saoirse. His flat was always springing leaks from The Orchard's very old lead pipes. Saoirse and I used to take turns to stop the flow of water, stabbing thumbs and fingers into the holes in the pipes, forever awaiting a plumber.

Around the mid-1980s, the old fellow in flat sixteen died and Jan moved in. Jan was a hero of the Polish resistance and inherited The Orchard longevity, living well into his nineties. Saoirse, frequently disturbed in the flat below, testified to a rather lively sex life. He was drably dressed and taciturn when you bumped into him in the foyer, 'an old misery' we all agreed. None of us were surprised that Jan's wife Maria had walked out many years ago. She had been, and indeed still was when you glimpsed her on the 65 bus, a beauty. Miss Polonia 1954, so they said. But something of the man who had charmed Maria as a young woman returned on social occasions. When, with some misgivings, I first invited Jan for Christmas drinks at number twelve, he dazzled. A touch of the 'lounge lizard' as my father used to put it. In his two-tone shoes and bow tie, you could see him schmoozing in some dodgy downtown bar.

I was only in his flat once. One snowy day I was doing my good neighbour thing by bringing bread and a few other basics. Jan invited me in. The flat was spotless. All the original thirties fittings were still in place. There seemed little by way of china or furnishings. There was, though, a rather beautiful art deco lamp and an ornate cabinet, which must have come with him from Poland. He went to the cabinet and took out two of four glasses, filling them with Polish vodka.

I had more to do with my neighbours in flat eighteen, directly above me. Dack and Holda appeared to be an ordinary enough couple, apart from their names, which always required justification on introduction – 'No, the vowels are right; we aren't Dick and Hilda or Jack and Dolly.' A good-looking pair. Holda was a beauty into old age, with her high cheekbones and striking white hair, coiled into a fetching pleat. Dack was past president of the Ealing Philanthropic Association and looked after the almshouses in Castlebar Park just round the corner from The Orchard. During the war, he had been in the Home Guard, made famous by the TV show *Dad's Army*. He had the look of Sergeant Wilson, the rather roué character played by John Le Mesurier. Dack was part of that bucolic scene which had confronted me on my first visit to The Orchard and was a passionate gardener.

In those days, there was a vegetable garden in The Orchard. Dack was in charge of this and very particular about his runner beans. His daughter Jackie, herself an expert gardener, tells me that, 'he would go to Uncle Harry's butcher in Hanwell to get fresh blood for the beans. Even better than the blood were fish and bones fertiliser packs. They gave the beans more flavour. And he would line the trenches with newspaper to hold in the water'.

But it was not just the vegetables, Jackie insists, when she and her sister Wendy, now in their eighties, come for annual Christmas gin and tonics at number twelve.

'Our father totally transformed the garden at The Orchard. I don't know what it's like now in spring and summer, but unless there are some keen resident gardeners, I doubt it looks as good. Dad made these wonderful compost heaps and left them for at least a year to mature, planting primroses on the top. I've never seen another gardener do that.'

Over the years, we've made efforts to restore the handiwork of those early gardeners. Gentle Laurie, the new gardener, recently enlisted by Harold and Eileen in flat seventeen, is doing his best. But Jackie is right. Since Dack died – suddenly of a heart attack, while buying fish down the Lane – the garden has never returned to its former glory.

THE PARTY YEARS

And if your dreams go nowhere
Don't give up the fight
Come with me and you will see
It all looks different in the morning light

From 'Things Can Only Get Better'

Labour Party campaign song, 1997

1981 to 1997

These were the party years. Some for Orchardians, like the annual Christmas drinks at number twelve, mainly for the Old-Timers. But others for my tech and university friends. The first 'sort of party' was when I moved in. Patricia, with whom I shared an office at the tech, and her then boyfriend Steve, my best friend Ruth Marks and Tom at number nine had organised a do-it-ourselves move from the famed 'bachelor flat' round the corner to my more spacious new home. As I recall, we transported my meagre belongings in Steve's camper van.

In the eighties and nineties, long before we had a thought of such matters as pandemics and all that came with this new reality in our lives, 'party' was a straightforward sort of word. Only much later were we led to ponder: when is a party not a party? A question that echoed across the land when, deep in the second phase of lockdown, Prime Minister Boris Johnson was accused of partying at Number 10 Downing Street, while we, in the rest of the country, were seeing only close family – or indeed no one, if we lived alone. The disputed incidents triggered debate about what might constitute a party – alcohol, planning, with proper invitations and… cake. Was even choice involved? Usually, we make a decision to go to something called a party – unlike a traffic accident, for instance – but even this requirement was called into question with claims that Johnson had been 'ambushed with a birthday cake'. He had 'happened upon' a party. 'Nothing to do with me, guv' type of thing.

In the early Orchard days, we were happy enough to describe a party as anything from a handful of people hanging out together, in an impromptu sort of way, to a highly organised 'do'. And of course there are sub genres: wakes are important kinds of parties, though most of these came later at The Orchard. Even wakes were banned in lockdown. Ironic, then, that one of Boris Johnson's many excuses for socialising was to support a staff 'leaving party', forgetting that a wake is the final and most significant of all leaving parties.

Once I had settled into The Orchard, there was a flow of parties, from sedate neighbourly gatherings to full-blooded shindigs, like the farewell for our students from the Soviet Union, leaving after an intensive ten-week English language course at the tech. And then, a few years later, my friend Noel's fiftieth birthday party. But also more earnest affairs, such as Saturday seminars with our students on multiculturalism and anti-racism, matters of deep concern to us – long before the Black Lives Matter movement became prominent. For this was the time of a growing interest in studies on racism and the black experience, especially as Ealing became more racially and socially diverse. Just a few years earlier, in 1974, Jessica and Eric Huntley, political activists, originally from British Guiana (later Guyana), had opened the Bogle-L'Ouverture Bookshop in an out-of-the-way cul-de-sac in Chignell Place, West Ealing, stocking books – and also publishing many – about the Caribbean, Africa and the Third World. Later renamed the Walter Rodney Bookshop, in honour of the Marxist African scholar who was murdered in Guyana, it became a cultural hub for the community, a 'drop-in centre' for parents, school students and teachers.

Gloria's knickers

One Orchard party, still talked about to this day, was the leaving do thrown in honour of the Russian students – as we tended to call them, though they were more properly Soviet, part of the then vast empire, stretching across Asia and Europe. My tech buddies were there: Barbara Sinclair, John Clegg, Patricia, Tom, our boss Brian Abbs and our new colleague Gloria. We'd all scrubbed up pretty well. But the night was Gloria's. She looked gorgeous. I remember the dress, green taffeta. It had a fifties look about it. Gloria bought all her frocks from a vintage stall in Portobello Road. The skirt was flared, the bodice tight, with a halter-style neckline. It was backless. The shoes were neat green courts. The knickers must have matched this carefully constructed outfit.

The Russians had offered to cook an Uzbek speciality called *plov*. How they managed to rustle this up in their miserable lodgings is a mystery. It's a dish that includes spiced lamb, whole heads of garlic, caramelised carrots, cumin and chillies. It takes three hours in the preparation and cooking. It was delicious, but there was loads left over. I recall hanging out my window the next day and saying to Tom in the garden below, 'Want any leftover *plov*?' Even better than the *plov* was the vodka. And not the wretched Smirnoff version that you mix with orange or lime juice. The authentic Russian version was always drunk neat. Pleading the cause of the promotion of international relations, Sasha, the leader of the group, had inveigled their embassy into supplying a generous quantity of the stuff. And we drank a lot. At some point there was a lively rendering of all The Beatles songs. As the night wore on, I have a memory of us swinging crazily round my living room in some pathetic version of a Cossack dance. The Russians looked on. They were unaccountably sober. At the end of the night, Gloria was as green as her beautiful dress. During one of the livelier dance routines, Brian had spilt vodka down her back and her knickers were soaked. She put them to dry on a radiator. The knickers disappeared and were long forgotten. I assumed they were still behind the radiator.

It was the spring of 1997. Barbara Sinclair was on a train from Moscow to Nizhny Novgorod. By now a well-known academic, she was returning from a conference on 'Crossroads of Culture' and was with a group of other academics on an overnight sleeper. No one could sleep. A crowd of Russians had also been at the conference and had decided to party. 'Come and join us,' they called to their comrades. So they did. In the course of a long night of carousing with vodka and sausage, Olga, the liveliest member of the group, disclosed that she had spent some time in Britain, 'in a place called Ealing'. Barbara could not recall Olga but mentioned the farewell party at The Orchard. 'I was there!' she cried. After many glasses of vodka, Barbara broached the matter of the lost knickers. Triumphant, Olga said, 'I know what happened to them!' Sasha had seen them drying on the radiator, pocketed them as a memento of the party, of the good times at Ealing and of the divine Gloria. Once back home at the Moscow Institute of Linguistics, he had pinned them to the wall of the staffroom. They remained there to that day.

Making *Morse*

Making *Morse* cannot count as a party exactly. Filming was on the morning of a funeral, that of my dear friend, Roger Andersen. It was only many years later that I felt able to watch, still available on the internet, the episode of *Morse* – 'Driven to Distraction' – which was shot in The Orchard on 8 September 1989. But for other residents, the occasion generated a lot of excitement: that we should have been chosen as a location for what was already an iconic TV series. That we might get to meet John Thaw, its famous star. We would be on the map. What's more, we were pleased that The Orchard received £500 – it's peanuts today – to go into the management fund, and my next-door neighbours received an equivalent sum for the inconvenience of being turfed out of their flat for the day. There had been some debate whether filming should be in my flat or number eleven next door. In the end, they had plumped for flat eleven, for no particular reason that I recall.

Many of the generic locations used throughout the

series, including Morse's house, were situated in Ealing, amongst the residential streets near The Orchard, to the north of Ealing Broadway. Though the days of Ealing comedies are long since gone, there is still a TV industry of local film-making. The vicarage next to St Peter's Church regularly turns up on *Midsummer Murders*. And the first murder in the *Morse* episode filmed at The Orchard takes place in a handsome turreted building just round the corner, in Castlebar Hill.

It was the echoey sound of feet on the unyielding surface of the long Orchard corridors that had particularly attracted the *Morse* site director – perfect, he thought, for the noir-ish scenes in 'Driven to Distraction'. Also the ghostly skylight. Later we put a carpet down – someone got it cheap from a hotel undergoing refurbishment – and the effect was ruined. The same director came back, wanting to use our flats for another *Morse* series that was being filmed in Ealing. 'What have you done?!' he shrieked, as he retreated down the corridor.

'Driven to Distraction', written by the acclaimed film director Anthony Minghella, features Derek, a seemingly harmless driving instructor who turns out to be a serial killer. The original art deco-style front doors of the flats in our building, and the skylight between the floors, are used to striking effect. Likewise the steel-clad iron banister at the far end of the long corridor, which soars upwards to the top floor. As I watch the episode again today, I note the addition of bars over the glass panes in the door of flat eleven to add, one assumes, to the sense of menace. The camera lurches dizzyingly as a young woman, clearly frightened out of her wits, comes to answer the insistent ringing of the doorbell.

The banister soaring upward

The key to the solution of the murders lies with the inhabitant of number eleven, a character called Phillipa Lao, though in the story the address that comes up on one of the early computers used by Morse is 7 The Orchard, Woodstock Road, Oxford. The Eurasian actress playing Ms Lao has little to say but is terrific at looking terrified. On three occasions Ms Lao comes to the door of her flat, looks through the spyhole and trembles with fear at what lies on the other side. The plot is full of red herrings and at least two of the mysterious figures at the door have little to do with the ultimate outcome of the story. One is a door-to-door salesman with an obscure foreign accent. Looming out of the darkness of the narrow corridor, he accosts a weeping Ms Lao as she tries to gain entry to her flat. 'Please read my card. I'm learning to sell things,' he intones. The final man at the barred window to flat eleven – number three by my count – is Inspector Morse himself. Not surprisingly, Ms Lao does not allow entry.

Phillipa Lao is the only woman who escapes with her life. Three others experience grisly deaths, all (as I can recognise from familiar streets) committed in their comfortable homes in the streets of leafy Ealing, masquerading as Oxford, the presumed location of all the Morse stories.

Things can only get better

The nineties brought a succession of parties to The Orchard. Most memorable was that for Noel Greig's fiftieth birthday. Noel, my boyfriend at university, had – along with my friend Ruth Marks and Jenny Harris – founded one of the first arts labs in the country, The Brighton Combination. Noel later became a well-known playwright and gay activist and, as one of my closest friends, was a frequent Orchard visitor until his death in 2009.

It was a time of chains and leather among gay men, and what I recall from the night of Noel's birthday party was the strange music of clanking and heavy boots coming down the long linoleumed corridor, which stops at my flat.

Noel – no surprise there – was a Christmas baby, born on Christmas Day 1944. So the famous party at The Orchard must have been in December 1994. A few years into John Major's seedy Tory government and beyond the dismal Thatcher years and all that had come with them.

What came with Thatcher of course, along with protest and upheaval on all fronts, was the miners' strike in 1985. Between March 1984 and March 1985, more than half the country's 187,000 miners left work in what was the biggest and most bitter industrial dispute in post-war Britain. The coal mines of Yorkshire, where the dispute began, and other mines from Kent to Wales were, one might suppose, a far cry culturally and geographically from suburban Ealing. But, along with university and college campuses across the land, we at Ealing Tech offered solidarity with the miners. At one fundraiser, Misty in Roots – a British reggae band, formed in the mid-1970s in Southall – played in the students' bar, which, a few years later – following Nelson Mandela's release from Robben Island – would be renamed Mandela Bar, along with a thousand student bars across the land.

And I remember the flurry of excitement when the young secretary of our branch of Ealing Labour Party announced – in her elegant, received pronunciation and in her elegant sitting room where we held ward meetings, in a rather posher, neighbouring block to The Orchard – 'We are twinning with a pit!' It was a time of a lot of twinning with all sorts of things. Barbara, my friend at Ealing Tech, scored an even bigger hit by contriving to host – in her front room in West Ealing – a group of miners from Dudley Pit. Like the story of the fashionable soirée at Leonard Bernstein's apartment, in which the wealthy elite of 1970s New York mingled with members of the Black Panther Party.

Barbara's little do was Ealing's version of 'radical chic'. I recall being envious that I had not thought of entertaining our comrades from the north in my own sitting room at The Orchard. Seen from the perspective of a more jaundiced modern era, long before the word 'woke' had been first used in African American vernacular English to mean 'alert to racial prejudice and discrimination' – before then being hijacked by the political right – we would have been considered naïve, even innocent.

And innocence is the word that comes to mind, when, more than a decade later, I found myself driving through Greenford with the Labour candidate for North Ealing in the 1997 general election. Steve Pound was very much the outsider in a safe Tory seat held by my Orchard neighbour Holda's favourite, Harry Greenaway. Steve was driving – for some reason I was also in the car – through the less prepossessing parts of Ealing. But the weather was balmy, and optimism and joy, even love, was in the air. You knew change was afoot.

Perhaps that is what brings to mind the idea of innocence: people ready to put their faith in something; a belief that has become unfashionable in more cynical times; a belief – dare I say it – in progress.

And of course we played the terrible song 'Things Can Only Get Better'. Passers-by waved, smiled. Someone turned to Steve and said, 'You're going to win this, Steve.' He looked terrified and puffed even harder on his cigarette.

Steve Pound won a landslide victory. Until his recent retirement, and defying the intervening vicissitudes, Pound was an extraordinarily popular MP for Ealing North, gaining massively greater majorities at each successive election. Steve's advice to a Labour Party colleague standing for the council was, 'Work the streets and wear a jacket.' And this is what Steve did. Being a local man helped. He had played football for Hanwell Town. He also did not come up through the political party machine. His Wikipedia entry tells us that he had been a boxer in the Merchant Navy when at sea from 1964–66, leading *Private Eye* magazine to refer to him as 'Ealing North's tattooed bruiser'. He had worked as a bus conductor for London Transport from 1966–68 and was a hospital porter from 1969–79. Later he worked for Paddington Churches Housing Association as a housing manager from 1984 until he became an MP. Once elected, Pound was ubiquitous. You would see him everywhere in Ealing, particularly in his home patch in Hanwell, working the streets and, yes, always smartly dressed. One day I saw him no fewer than three times – on the tube coming into Ealing Broadway, later haring down Greenford Avenue and at a branch meeting in the evening.

As many will testify, the Labour victory of 1997 cannot be appreciated without an understanding of the years, decades even, of pain that preceded it. Noel, Patricia, Barbara and others slumped morose in front of the telly in my living room, inured to disappointment, with each defeat further bruised by failure. On the morning after the Labour rout of 1992, Noel left a large note in his distinctive curvy handwriting. He was always leaving notes as he disappeared. 'I'm wearing my Lenin badge,' he said.

Over many years, election parties became a tradition in The Orchard. Well, if I'm honest, probably only at number twelve. For these were still the Tory years at The Orchard and in Ealing. As a stalwart Labour Party supporter, I knew all the candidates for Ealing North, which was at that time my parliamentary constituency: Hilary Benn, for a time an Ealing councillor, ran as Labour candidate for Ealing North. Bob Malloy, later Lord Malloy, actually held the seat for a few years, until the long reign of Harry Greenaway. On that famous night in May 1997, the night Blair actually made it, Noel, Patricia and others who had shared the years of dashed hopes were there. My brother and I hugged and roared. We danced along with the nation, rejoicing in what later became known as 'the Portillo moment'. The Portillo moment was the dramatic declaration of the result for the Enfield Southgate constituency election, at around three o'clock in the morning, when the Conservative cabinet minister, Michael Portillo, unexpectedly lost his seat to a startled-looking stripling politician called Stephen Twigg.

The Labour victory party

My boss at the tech, Brian Abbs – who'd campaigned hard all his life for the Labour Party – would answer the phone during the halcyon early months of the Blair government with the words, 'new Labour, new dawn!'

A Labour victory merited another party at The Orchard. The tech crowd – all socialists of various shades of pink and red – turned up. Barbara and Gloria, now the closest of buddies, in matching outfits. We'd exploited Gloria's glamour shamelessly on the campaign trail, I remember, pinning a giant Labour rosette on her splendid bosom, as we led her from door to door, like a prize pony.

Tom was there. I'd lost touch with him for a few years after he left The Orchard but had bumped into him down the Broadway. Factions were shelved, old enmities forgotten. Times were good.

THREE FUNERALS

Jan, war hero, so they said,
The last of many, long since dead.

From 'Ode to Jan' by Cathie Wallace

2000-2020

While the first two decades of my Orchard years offered occasions for partying, from around the time of the millennium came the deaths of some of The Orchard's Old-Timers. The first funeral was that of Jan Bukowski, the Polish war hero who had lived in flat sixteen for many years.

The last of many

Jan Bukowski had quarrelled with close family and pretty much everyone else. But when he was very ill, Maria, from whom he had been divorced for forty years, went every day to sit with him in the elegant ex-servicemen's home in Castlebar Park.

'It's my duty,' she said.

Andrzej and I represented The Orchard at the funeral. Maria was there with her only son (not the estranged daughter) and six old soldiers. A woman in a pew just inside the door of the cavernous Polish Catholic Church of Our Lady Mother of the Church sobbed quietly throughout.

My experience of this last ritual in our lives had been limited to rather perfunctory services, which made only a nod to religious belief, as well as some wonderful ones which were funny and full of character. Jan's funeral at the Polish Church on the Broadway was different; certainly Catholic (Jan was devout) but a bleak affair. Nothing personal, nothing about the man beyond his exemplary war service. I struggled to follow the order of service, shamed that I had never learnt a word of Polish, when to all intents and purposes, Ealing is a Polish town. I was moved. I even wrote a poem.

Ode to Jan

Ten, I counted ten, some women, mainly men.
Jan, war hero, so they said,
The last of many, long since dead.
We sit, still, numb, no laughter, tears.
The wife, estranged for many years,
Still handsome, but alone.
No daughter (she is mentioned), just a son.

A single voice, clear, simple, strong.
A tape perhaps? But no, I'm wrong.
The singer sits aloft, the sweet voice soars
Beyond all thought of conflict, wars.

Jan, bloody-minded, that we know,
Curmudgeonly, a boor, but even so,
Where are the lovers, comrades, friends

Who might have come to make amends?
The daughter, what's the story there?
I rise and sit and rise – a stranger here.

A youngish woman, head in hand.
As we troop out, a ragged band.
She weeps, tears flow, but not, I think, for Jan.

A few weeks after the funeral, Maria brought to my
door at The Orchard the four glasses and the lamp, which I
had admired in Jan's flat that snowy day some years earlier.

It's all true

Present at Jan's funeral was Andrzej, also known as
Andrew. For as long as I can remember, he has been
part of Orchard life. He was certainly not around when
I arrived in the eighties, but from the turn of the century,
everything has hinged on Andrzej. Unlike T.S. Eliot's
Macavity the Mystery Cat, he is *always* there.

Andrzej's demeanour is impressive. The flowing white
hair. The stylish hat, worn winter or summer; the heavy
Loden coat so that he looks as though he has just come
down from the Russian steppe. Emil at flat fourteen, also
Polish, tells me that his family is aristocracy, though a
notch down from himself, adds Emil, who claims even
grander lineage, in turn, it must be said, denied by Andrzej.
'Kowalski is just Smith in Polish,' says Andrzej.

Each year I tease Andrzej about his monogrammed
slippers, as he greets us at the AGM of The Orchard
management company, which takes place at his home just
round the corner from The Orchard, on the Brentham
Estate. In the early days, I tended to look askance at Andrzej

and his wife, Ewa. Our politics were very different for a start. On election day, their handsome property bristles with Conservative posters and stakes – emblazoned with the famous Tory oak tree logo – driven firmly into an exquisitely landscaped garden.

Around the time that Andrzej and Ewa came into our lives, Kim Thorne turned up. I no longer remember when or how. But once ensconced in The Orchard, Kim was ubiquitous; a shambling figure, with sparse, sandy-coloured hair, trousers at half mast, often nursing a can of Special Brew. He had a flat in Shepherd's Bush, but during the day, he took up residence in a shed in our garden. He appeared to be in the pay of Andrzej and Ewa, picking up odd jobs here and there. I thought of Kim as Andrzej's 'creature' – the comic relief in a Jacobean or Shakespearean play: the porter in *Macbeth*; Bardolph in *Henry V*; even the fool to Andrzej's Lear.

Kim enjoyed telling the story of Andrzej walking down Whitehall wearing, Kim claimed, fake medals, side by side with the real Polish war heroes. Another story has it that one day, as Kim was eating in his favourite Polish restaurant in Hammersmith, 'Andrzej walks in and says he has just bought the restaurant'.

These stories are almost certainly mischievous fabrications by Kim. Nonetheless, Andrzej's credentials are impressive. Over the years in our garden storytelling, we continue to debate the extent of Andrzej's virtuosity. Can he really be a champion Formula One racing driver, an acclaimed published writer of military history and a professor of engineering at UCL? One evening in lockdown, Emil and I revisit the puzzle over a glass of whisky.

Emil: 'When my father was still alive. Knock at the door. Andrzej had been hunting.'

Cathie: 'Hunting? What was he hunting?'

E: 'Pheasants. He just showed up. He looked like Hermann Goering, with two pheasants. They weren't actually that bad. Andrzej being Andrzej, he launched into another story. He'd just bought an E-boat – you go out to get a loaf of bread and he buys a German E-boat. This is from the war... and he does have a Mercedes 150. It's the same one that Grace Kelly drove in *High Society*.'

C: 'You're kidding.'

E: 'Well not the same one – the same *kind* of car. He has taken part in the Monte Carlo Rally. These are not idle claims.'

C: 'He says he's a professor at UCL and he's a champion racing driver and... I mean how can that *all* be true?'

E: 'The stories are all true. Improbable as it may sound, they're all true. What he says, it's all true.'

The stories are not only true but do less than justice to some aspects of Andrzej's life. One evening when we are at last able to socialise after the third lockdown, Andrzej fills me in, as we share an expensive bottle of Claret. Although now well off, as a young man not long arrived from Poland, recently married and still completing his doctorate, Andrzej was short of cash and found himself working for a fellow émigré Pole – Perec, or Peter, Rachman.

Rachman was an extremely nasty character, West London's answer to the East End Kray twins. He became notorious for the exploitation of his tenants, with the word 'Rachmanism' entering the Oxford English Dictionary as a synonym for exploitation and intimidation, especially of the West Indian population who rented many of the rundown properties owned at that time by Rachman in Notting Hill. During our conversation, Andrzej makes no bones about how contemptible his employer was. Though on the fringes of this world, Andrzej met a number of Peter Rachman's henchmen and lovers, which included two iconic figures of the sixties, Christine Keeler and Mandy Rice-Davies.

'When I went to King's College to do my PhD, I was a foreign student. Two years after we got married, there was an advert in the *Evening Standard* – they were looking for an electrician in Battersea. At the time, you could import one-armed bandits from America and they'd been bringing in shiploads, but they needed to be converted. So I applied for the job… met two guys, the second one kind of English but with a Polish accent. That was Rachman. There was also this guy Serge, Hungarian, painter – still around, he lives in South Kensington. It was Serge who showed me the white Cadillac with two Alsatians and Mandy Rice-Davies in the front and – at the back – Christine Keeler.'

Andrzej's racier connections are long in the past. A few years ago, as testimony to the work he does with the Polish community, he was presented with an MBE. He shows us Orchard folk the pictures with his handsome daughters and wife, elegantly turned out. And he tells the story of how, in his words, Princess Anne, standing in for the Queen on this occasion, 'waved away all the others' (Andrzej acts this out affectingly) to pay proper attention to himself.

One lunchtime a few years ago, Andrzej came sweeping into my living room, in response to a call for help. There was a minor disaster. The sweet but ditsy young women – they preceded the Wild Girls – who lived below me at the time, were always parking in front of my garage, and I couldn't get my car out to take my American friend Elsa to the airport. The macho attempts of James and Andrzej to shift the car were fruitless – in the end we had to take a cab. But Elsa was charmed when, like an old-fashioned European aristocrat, Andrzej bowed deeply on his arrival in my flat and kissed her hand. He may even have clicked his heels.

The old oak

Unlike Elsa, Holda at flat eighteen was deeply suspicious of Andrzej's continental ways. The oleaginous charm cut no ice. 'I feel I should lock up my china,' she said darkly on one occasion, when he had called round for a cup of tea. This despite the fact that Andrzej adored Holda and his impromptu visit was possibly motivated by a wish to support someone he saw as a lonely widow – an identity Holda would have spurned.

After her husband Dack's sudden death one beautiful autumn day, Holda lived on for many years, in buoyant good health.

She was suspicious of change. A natural Conservative, loyal to Harry Greenaway, the Tory MP for North Ealing for eighteen years. Just before the famous 1997 election, Holda was scathing about the possibility of a Labour government, whenever I popped up to her flat for afternoon tea or stiff gins at Christmas with her stepdaughters, Wendy and Jackie. I remember talking to her about Tony Blair's arrival on the political scene. She considered Blair a lightweight, an arriviste. 'He looks terrified,' she said. She was an intelligent and highly capable person who had held a responsible job running day nurseries in the borough of Ealing. Not at all a person to be intimidated or phased by anything. Still, she is likely to have felt the effects of a shift in the mood of the times. The feeling of solidity, continuity, permanence, was eroding. As The Orchard Old-Timers died off, the New Cosmopolitans arrived, younger, more socially liberal, more mobile – expecting to move back and forth to Europe and, further, across the globe. Afternoon tea would become Prosecco in the garden, Burns nights, summer barbecues.

Change at The Orchard reflected a change in Ealing and London more widely. The Polish character of Ealing – always present – became more dominant, but distinctively different too, with new waves of Poles arriving, some less educated than earlier cohorts so that there was a class distinction within the community. Pretty well everyone now comes from somewhere else. At The Orchard, over the years, I can count over twenty nationalities: South African, Australian, Bulgarian, Cape Verdean, Zambian, Nigerian, Indian, Irish, Polish, Iranian, Sri Lankan, Portuguese, French, Italian, Greek, Jamaican, Hungarian, Latvian, Slovenian, Japanese, Chinese, Russian, Argentinian. I'm sure there are more, those who came and went so quickly I hardly had time to say 'hello'.

Holda must have been disappointed also at the neglect of the garden after Dack had died. The pristine vegetable and flower beds, deprived of the army of devoted workers, faded and died.

When Andrzej threatened to cut down the old oak in The Orchard garden, it was Holda's idea that we should chain ourselves to the tree in protest. She probably wasn't entirely serious. She always had a sense of humour. However, ever suspicious of Andrzej's motives, she felt that his primary concern was that the tree, clearly a bit doddery, might fall on his Mercedes, perhaps even on the one we called 'the Grace Kelly' one – the one identical to the car she drove in *High Society* and part of a fleet of cars Andrzej parked by the garages out the back. We lost the battle and the tree went. It was on its last legs and almost certainly a lost cause. We planted a new young oak, carefully nurtured by Andrzej over the years. To this day, he and I have intense discussions as to how to keep it alive, after some particularly unpleasant neighbours – they didn't stay long – hammered nails into its delicate trunk in an attempt to improvise a washing line.

When Holda knew she was dying, she turned to me and said, 'I hear things are not very good "out there".' She meant in the world beyond Charing Cross Hospital. It was 2003, memorable for some of us as the start of the Iraq War and the subsequent loss of trust in Tony Blair. Later in the year, there was a famous heatwave. But, compared to the more recent horrors of the financial crisis, Brexit and Covid, and war in the heart of Europe, daily life for most of us was manageable.

What Holda probably meant was that she was ready to go. And hers was a good death. Her final illness from cancer was brief and she was in great nick well into her eighties. Elegant in her pussy bow blouses and trim trouser suits until her last few months, she was regularly spotted dashing down to the Broadway to get her groceries, her trolley bouncing behind.

Her funeral brought one last small surprise. I had always called her Holda, but she was in fact Hulda, Hulda Lucy Fryer, née Ogden. Hulda's maiden name was close to that of the famous *Coronation Street* character Hilda Ogden, though our Hulda is unlikely to have been a fan of the popular TV soap.

Leopard-skin slippers

When Hulda died, glamorous Elena Edwards bought her flat, above mine at number eighteen, and indeed, over time, a few of the other flats. She came with two vicious little dogs, which bit people's ankles, and she claimed a number of identities of uncertain provenance. Through marriage, she was a Polish countess as well as a high-powered city lawyer, an interior designer, a successful businesswoman, much as the fancy took her. The grudging affection of my Polish neighbours for each other did not extend to Elena, as Andrzej notes, during his reminiscences to me:

'She's a disaster. I knew her when she was with husband number one – or was it number two? I had the pleasure of meeting her son… he was highly unpleasant. I've seen how she treated her husband – not sure which one, either number three or four. She was totally irresponsible. I was always trying to stop her flooding your place. She used stupid plumbers. I had to call Pimlico Plumbers many times. She was a completely selfish, irresponsible type of person. She just used all these men.'

Andrzej has a point: Elena operated rather like a local gang master with groups of casually employed Polish workers in her pay, at one point housing most of them in number eighteen while she moved next door to flat seventeen. At that time, she also ran a tanning salon down the Broadway. Her hair was tastefully blonde, her skin an impressive Donald Trump-style bronze – in fairness, more subtly achieved. After a day in the salon, she would often trip down the shabby Orchard back stairs in her leopard-skin, kitten-heel slippers for a gossip and a glass of wine at my place. She claimed to have had many affairs, some with people I knew. Discretion does not, however, permit disclosure – lips are firmly sealed. What is certain is that, as Andrzej recalled, she had at least four husbands. The first was the Polish count and then a property developer in the home counties. The third was very brief, a much younger guy; the fourth was Anton. Not much was known about Anton. He dyed his hair a rather spectacular red. 'So much better to have kept the natural grey,' said Eileen in flat seventeen, who kept a close watch on the comings and goings of Elena's husbands and lovers, across the back stairway.

Fuelled by massive consumption of white wine in my flat, Elena confided in me about her affairs, the wayward son, her ongoing feuds with Kim, Jan and Andrzej. At various times she fell out with all of them. She and I maintained an uneasy friendship, even though I would regularly come back after Christmas to find water pouring through my kitchen ceiling, as Andrzej observed. This perturbed Elena not a jot. She would get her troupe of Polish workers (decorators is too grand a term) to patch things up. When I pointed out the botched result – not surprising as they were paid starvation wages – she would cry, 'drunk again! All drunk!' as she flounced off.

Elena has long since retreated to the Costa del Sol with Anton. I miss the sound of her leopard-skin slippers on the back stairs and the times, well into the night, she held court with various admirers on summer evenings in The Orchard garden. I miss her vicious lapdogs.

After Elena left, The Orchard became full of children. Once off to Marbella, Elena had let out her top-floor flat first to a Japanese couple with a tiny boy who made an impressive amount of noise, nonetheless exemplary neighbours, followed by Lita and Herve and their beautiful son Matthias. And in flat six beneath me there was a similar procession of children: a lovely Iranian couple with their boy, Alborz: trilingual, brilliantly successful at his primary school, keen Chelsea supporter, a fledgling citizen of the world. Then two sets of twins. First, teenagers, Jerry and Sam, whose parents were Len, of Caribbean heritage, and Joan, a white woman from Swindon. Andrzej reminds me that the Tufts, the neighbours who had mutilated the oak tree, had fallen out with Len over some matter so trivial that one suspected racism on the part of the Tufts. Later came twin girls, very 'advanced' – which meant they were allowed to draw all over the walls. Their parents were very quarrelsome, with each other and all the neighbours. I had to intervene one time in an argument over a vegetable. I think it was a marrow.

Much later came Becky and Leonard with their boys, Olly and Matt, who raced around the garden with Matthias, or played on the back stairs. Becky and Leonard were niche photographers. Leonard specialised in photographing politicians and had deliciously salacious and mostly unrepeatable stories about some of them. Becky gained considerable success in photographing naked pregnant women. The genre became very fashionable a few years ago, following a famous image – taken not by Becky but by an American photographer – of an expectant Demi Moore, which was featured on the cover of *Vanity Fair*.

Adventurer, soldier, schoolmaster, traveller

It was during this time that The Orchard lost another old warrior. Gerald Horrocks. Gerald and Jeanne Horrocks had moved some years earlier to a smart detached house round the corner. But we kept in touch with them and

Gerald had a decent turnout for his funeral when he was well over ninety.

I had thought the Horrocks the archetypal pillars of the community. But Gerald had a raffish past. In the commemorative order of service, his son William described him as 'adventurer, soldier, schoolmaster, traveller, fluent in Greek, Arabic and Swahili'. Another son tells us that Gerald was 'a legendary president of the Old Durstonian Association'. There were hints in the eulogy of an ill-advised early marriage, exotic adventures in Greece and Africa, until he courted and married Jeanne. The order of service revealed that Gerald Horrocks was more properly Captain Thomas Gerald Capper Horrocks, Captain with the British Army in East Africa. An old black-and-white photograph shows a handsome chap, something of a ladies' man, with a pencil-thin moustache, firm jaw, steady gaze and Brylcreemed hair. His son's funeral eulogy tells us that he 'fearlessly explored the work of technological innovation, mastering first the camcorder and then the computer'.

It was at the funeral that we found out that the woman we had always known as *Jeanne* was in fact *Claudine*. With a name like 'Claudine', there must surely have been a life beyond the Ealing Historical Association or the bowling club. At the least, one feels, someone called 'Claudine' must have worked for the French resistance during the Second World War. She would have looked good in a beret, on a bike.

ANOTHER FUNERAL, AND A WEDDING

'Ealing born and bred,' you said,
Talented, well versed, well read.
You knew the score
And much, much more.

From 'Tribute to Kim Thorne' by Cathie Wallace

2000-2020

There is a pattern at The Orchard by which people move from flat to flat. Hazel and Jack moved three times, as their family grew bigger. Ivan, at one time in Tom's old flat, turned up in flat twenty a few years later with a new partner Maggie and their two little daughters Clara and Octavia. As a single woman, Hulda had lived in number nine before moving to the more spacious flat eighteen, after she married Dack. Emil Kowalski was part of this movement, relocating from number nine to an identical flat, just across the first-floor corridor.

Emil and Kim

For years I barely knew Emil. He was the tall, exotic-looking chap who lived at the end of the corridor, not much in evidence at The Orchard as he travelled round the world. Something called 'troubleshooting' I think. Emil looks very much like the BBC art critic – so much so that a cab driver insisted on one occasion that it was indeed Will Gompertz. I realised the error (the resemblance is striking) and demurred. My cabbie friend wasn't having it. 'No, of course it's him. He's on the telly. He's in my cab pretty well every night.'

Emil says how he arrived at The Orchard in 1997, around the time of the great Labour victory. First as Andrzej's tenant in flat nine, before his move over the corridor into number fourteen.

Certainly, Emil hadn't been at Hulda's funeral, nor at Jan's. He may have been travelling. He became close to Becky and Leonard, once they turned up in flat six, and must have coincided with Elena, but I think they had little to do with each other. His elegant manners would have endeared him to her, though it is likely he would have thought her a touch nouveau riche. It was only when I decided, on a whim, one Christmas to invite all the neighbours to drinks that he arrived at my door with a bottle of very expensive champagne, before dashing back down the corridor. 'Can't stay but love the idea of the party.'

Emil and Kim became mates. Emil – elegantly dressed, sophisticated – Kim – rough and ready, with an indeterminate West London accent, definitely not posh like his friend, a view which would be challenged by Andrzej some time later. Kim and Emil would share a tandoori on a Friday night at Monty's down the Broadway. I joined them one night and was surprised how well Kim scrubbed up. Smart shirt, handsome tie, well-combed hair.

Ealing is full of restaurants called Monty's – the original Monty, Mahanta Shrestha, came to the UK in the late 1970s and his Nepalese restaurant became so popular that when the management decided to go their separate ways, they all agreed to keep the name. Our favourite Monty's, and the one patronised by Kim and Emil, is the one just past Ealing Broadway tube, on the Uxbridge Road.

Kim was a bit of a wheedler and a flatterer. He said my coffee was better than Becky's downstairs. I fell for this, and almost daily, Kim came wheezing up the back stairs for a fag, coffee, gossip and, always, lots of Ealing stories. He'd been, for a time, in the music business and, with the proprietorial air he assumed about all Orchard matters, took it upon himself to research the old story about Fleetwood Mac's residence in number twelve. Sadly, he drew a blank. While professing liberal, even leftish, views, Kim could come across as an awful old racist, having a go at the Polish regulars who did much of the serious work around The Orchard. He claimed to be a Communist, though this might just have been a way to ingratiate himself with Emil, who has posters of Che Guevara, Fidel Castro and Rosa Luxemburg on the kitchen wall.

Behind the 'rough diamond' persona Kim presented at first sight, was a cultured hinterland. At one point he'd worked for Reuters, so Andrzej said. His love of books and reading and Emil's handsome objets d'art was genuine.

His appreciation of the wine that Eileen and Harold always gave him for Christmas confirmed a taste for the finer things of life. So we shouldn't have been surprised when he turned his hand to more ambitious projects than fixing the odd drainage problem. He made my bookcases, one in honour of my mother, containing her modest collection of favourites; a second dedicated to my friend Noel. At the same time, Kim ingeniously refashioned a third, older bookcase, made originally by my father, carefully matching the wood, so as to fit in with the bookcases he had built from scratch.

Kim was a patcher-upper; he patched up my walls and ceiling, stained with successive floods from Elena's flat upstairs. He patched up the original 1930s cistern. He was an expert in keeping the old loo going. And when, after many hours with his head down my lavatory bowl, Kim finally conceded defeat, he knew just where to take the cistern – to the Hanwell and Ealing Heritage Museum. No one had ever heard of this. But Kim had local knowledge. 'Ealing born and bred,' he always said – and sure enough, there is the tiny museum on the website, based in Hanwell Community Centre. Few people in Hanwell, let alone further afield, know of its existence.

Emil tells the story of his introduction to Kim:

Brilliance and bungling

'I asked Andrzej if he knew of anyone who could assemble a giant CD storage unit and was pleased to hear that we had appointed "a new building manager and carpenter". *Perfect*, I thought. So I wasn't prepared for the shambling Falstaffian figure who knocked on my door the next day. He was dressed like a large bag of clothes destined for a charity shop.

'However, I was quickly exposed to Kim's brilliant idiot savant approach to construction and his storytelling gifts.

'After I had observed that he had assembled the unit, leaving both multiple screws and bolts left over and the legs unattached, he paused and quickly pronounced that this was in fact the latest Scandinavian interior design style. It would look better and be easier to hoover.

'I was impressed by the speed and originality of his thought, linguistic flair and a dislike – which I shared – of interiors looking like BMW showrooms and Kim embarked on several projects in my flat, with execution continuing to straddle the line between brilliance and bungling. He designed an art deco-style fireplace for the living room. Impressive – or it would have been had not he run out of wood so that the artfully produced buttresses on each side of the fireplace were oddly unbalanced.

'The kitchen was next to be subject to Kim's critical gaze. The results were spectacular until, on closer inspection, I found a kitchen shelving unit had been installed with a gap of five inches. Without missing a beat, he pointed out it was the perfect width for a wine rack. He'd just been waiting to discuss the idea with me.

'When I'd stopped laughing, I agreed that this deserved a special "thank you" and so arranged to meet at the Soho bar of a landlord friend of his to repay him. The afternoon continued (descended?) into a pub crawl of Greek and Dean Streets and culminated in a row in the Pillars of Hercules with a former Doctor Who over the merits of lettuce.

'Some time later, at a football match, I received an automated phone call after my cleaner, Brzoska, had activated the alarm in my flat while hoovering. Having installed the system with a hair trigger, Kim had created the following message:

'*This is Kim. You are being burgled. Hope you hid the vintage champagne.*

'In true Kim style, the alarm couldn't be deactivated

and James had to rip it from the wall and smash it with a hammer to switch it off.'

A favourite of the many Kim stories is one that had us all concerned at The Orchard. The time Kim went missing. Emil tells the often-repeated story, one which, it must be said, is embellished with each retelling:

When Kim went missing

Emil: 'Three or four years ago, Andrzej rang me up in a state of tremendous excitement. He'd asked Kim on a Wednesday to meet him, but he couldn't get in touch with him and then on the Thursday he tried again to get in touch with him... and at this stage Andrzej was getting worried. On the Friday someone thought he'd gone out to some of his drinking dens.'

Cathie: 'Like the Black George.'

Emil: 'I was tired, and I didn't think too much about it and then I *did* start to think about it. No one had seen him for three or four days. By now Andrzej was beginning to get really worried. I had come back to The Orchard. I was working Monday to Thursday in Leeds and Andrzej rang me up again in a state of mental excitement, saying, "I don't know where Kim is."

'"Well, have you rung him?"

'"Yes." Part of it was that Andrzej didn't want to go over to his house. I'm not even sure he knew where his house was. And I said, "Shall I go and find out if Kim's there." So I went. It was getting quite late.

'Andrzej was quite scared, thinking what we'd find if we went to his apartment. So I made my way... I found out where it was eventually. It's a thirties block, but no one seemed to be speaking to each other. Getting in and out required a huge amount of effort. The arrangement was… they had three neighbours in very close proximity. Knocked on Kim's door. Couldn't see anything but there appeared to be a light on. And I thought, *this is not looking good*. So I banged on his neighbour's door. One was out. Two were out. The third said, "I haven't seen him since Tuesday."

'I said to Andrzej over the phone, I said, "I think there might be a problem," and he replied, "We need to call the police," and I agreed. So I contacted the police. It's amazing how quickly they turned up… it must have been a slow day for crime in London. And they arrived and they wanted to take my details. By this stage we were starting to gather a bit of a crowd. Kim lived, technically, in East Acton, more Shepherd's Bush, just down from Wormwood Scrubs. It's quite a nice block, but it's running to seed.

'By this stage I was getting really worried because I thought, *there's a light on, no one's seen him since Tuesday*. I could see the post on the mat. *There's going to be a dead body the other side*, I thought. Anyway, this cop takes a run-up, and after a couple of whacks, the door comes down. It's amazing how easily the cops can break a door down when they need to. I won't say I'm shaking, but I'm thinking the worst.

'I follow the cops in. No Kim. Flat a bit dishevelled. It's a very spartan life he led. But no indication of where he is.'

James arrives at this point and Emil updates him on the story…

'This is the story when Kim went missing. We just got to the bit where the cops broke down the door and I really expected… there appeared to be a light on, the post hadn't been collected. No one had seen him since Tuesday.

I expected to see a body there. The cops went there. Then they frantically reassembled the door. A police crime scene. Then questions, questions, questions. But we were still none the wiser – where is he? – and I had to give all sorts of details. And we were really worried by this stage. He had a relative in the West Country, that's all. His car was here at The Orchard, but inoperable.

'Anyway. This is about lunchtime on Saturday, we are alone with our thoughts and then – suddenly – about six o'clock, the phone rings.

'"Kim here. They've knocked down my fucking door!"

'I never got to the bottom of what he'd done. I didn't want to probe. I think there'd been an amazing bender, and he decided he didn't want to speak to Andrzej.

'And then he found that the Met will only stump up the first few hundred quid to replace a door. Kim being Kim, he was able to put the door back on its hinges somehow, but it was a typical Kim botched job, very hard to get in and out, but there you are. That's…'

James: '…the saga of Kim.'

Another door

This story often segues into another 'door' story, which Emil also loves to tell. This time the door was my own front door – also, like Kim's, broken down by the police.

I had arrived home late one morning to find my front door wide open and the reassuring but puzzling presence of my niece Kate, profiled in the doorway at the end of the long corridor. The stylish dark bob, the pale oval face outlined against the light from my hall window.

I have a small army of nieces, and the niece network had been in overdrive that morning. A company called

Bluebird Care, whom I'd asked to help out as I'd broken my arm, not finding me at home, had, overzealously, contacted family members. There had been frantic phone calls to my doctor niece who had said – not so reassuringly – that a collapse in the shower was surprisingly common and often fatal. Kate, my oldest niece, in a school where she works as a speech therapist in East London, felt that she had no choice but to hotfoot it from the other side of the city to Ealing to check things out, calling the police on the way. By the time she arrived, the police had already smashed the door down and my diary, open on the bed, revealed an appointment at Ealing Hospital.

Not that long ago, Ealing Hospital Trust was – before a later merger with North West London Hospitals – listed bottom out of the 165 trusts in England in a survey of patients' ratings of the level of care. Leading to much gallows humour among local residents. Even the appearance of the place is less than prepossessing. My American friend Elsa was scathing when I pointed out the gloomy, gulag-like building on the Uxbridge Road. It is perhaps no accident that exterior shots for the BBC black comedy on hospital life, Adam Kay's *This Is Going to Hurt* were filmed at Ealing Hospital, where Kay previously worked before he wrote his famous diaries about the National Health Service. Many fans have visited the site hoping to find a memorial tree, which was planted for a young doctor, Shruti, who – as portrayed in Kay's TV show – takes her own life. Recently, I found the spot and the commemorative plaque just under the tree. Shruti was a fictional character, but the memorial honours the many healthcare workers who have succumbed to the pressure of their role. It reads:

Shruti's Tree
In memory of healthcare professionals who
have died by suicide.
Take care of those who take care of others.

Perhaps protectively, we Ealingites are loyal to our local hospital, and I've had only excellent treatment with a variety of medical complaints. In fact, it was because of their efficiency that I got out of the hospital early that morning – the arm was healing well – and dropped by to see my friend Patricia in Hanwell, just over the road from the hospital, so failing to be back in time to save my front door.

The only difficulty I've had at the hospital is with my identity. About five years ago, the brisk receptionist said – accusingly, in response to my RP-ish accent, as though I was trying to get one over on someone – 'You don't sound as though you need an interpreter.' Some weeks later, I was similarly accosted by a further administrator. 'It says here that you need an interpreter.' This time, mischievously, I tuned up my middle-class voice in reply, at which my interlocuter dissolved in giggles.

Eventually, the note of my need for an interpreter did leave my NHS record. But more recently, when I turned up with another minor health problem, I was down as 'White Irish'. This happened a couple of times, until I demurred. 'Well, you are called Wallace,' one doctor said helpfully, even though Wallace is a Scottish name. When I tried again, I was told – pleasantly but firmly – 'It's very hard to make any change on the system.' So for a time, I gave up. Until I resolved the situation by applying for an Irish passport. With my father born in Ireland, I had been

Irish all along, without knowing it. Now – with Brexit in place – it meant that I could claim a European identity, in addition to my newly discovered Irish one. It also meant that I could happily call myself 'White Irish', in compliance with my hospital records.

On the day of the door, Kate and I had a brandy. Then we put the incident behind us. However, it remains a story Emil loves to recount. The numbers of policemen and their haplessness increase with each telling. Latterly, a policewoman has been added. The guys were trying to impress her, says Emil. I've never liked to ask why on earth Emil did not stop them breaking down the door. Why did he just stand there? Eventually, I had to pay a fortune for a bespoke job. What we had thought to be perfectly ordinary doors turned out to be unique in size, the panes of glass in the windows a very distinctive shape. A replacement could be no off-the-shelf job – we all agreed that we wanted to keep the art deco-ish feel to the building. A new door had to be made to order by a skilled craftsman. In the end, after much sleuthing, we found a very elderly local Irish carpenter, Harry, supported by his wife Maureen.

Weeks later, the new door was carried aloft down the corridor. Harry and Maureen, a slightly built blonde, struggled with its bulk. But it was a thing of beauty. Even the secluded Jannis, who rarely emerged from flat ten, came out to watch. Emil thought he might ask Harry to make one for him, though his existing door was perfectly adequate. It's true that the wood was beautiful – much better than the fairly cheap original stuff. However, despite the stalwart efforts of Harry and Maureen, the new door never quite fitted, and a great draught of air now whistled through the flat. It also had a very large keyhole, facilitating my spying on the corridor comings and goings during the darkest days of lockdown.

The red hand of Ulster and other tales

James, like Emil and Kim, is a skilled storyteller. The humour drier, quieter than Emil's, perhaps more subtle, helped by his soft Irish accent. He was at school in Northern Ireland with Sammy Wilson, the DUP politician. So why has James got a voice you could fall in love with? Why doesn't he sound like Wilson, whose accent is like a chainsaw driving through your skull?

When in the mood, James will share experiences of schooling at his boys' grammar school in Belfast. A favourite is of one teacher whose enthusiasm for corporal punishment was evident on the boys' backsides for weeks. The consequences of Miss Foster's labour came to be known as 'the red hand of Ulster'. The red hand appears everywhere in the folklore of Northern Ireland and even today can be seen on some of the many flags flying in the city of Belfast. The origin of the story is shrouded in mystery, so James tells us. However, popular legend has it that, back in pagan times, in the race to capture the kingship of Ulster, the first man to lay his hand on the province would have claim to it. This led one man to chop off his hand and throw it over the heads of his comrades. The bloody hand landed on the disputed territory before his rivals were able to reach land by boat.

James is probably best at the travel tales. He kayaks in all weathers and all over the British Isles, often in the Solent, perhaps a bit less now that Simone has moved in with him at number thirteen. He tells the story, which brings to mind Coleridge's famous ballad of 'The Rime of the Ancient Mariner', of how a few years ago he kayaked from Land's End to the Isles of Scilly:

'We kayaked from Land's End to the Isles of Scilly. Several years ago... we headed out to – there's a lighthouse just there. The day we went, there was a funny mist on the sea. There's a shipping lane. We got through that OK.

'And then we thought, *where are the Scillies?* They should be on the horizon. We knew we were somewhere close, but we couldn't see a darn thing. And the sea was grey. There was a kind of grey sky, and there was a grey horizon. It all sort of melted into one. I said to the others, "We're just about there, boys." But we couldn't see a darn thing. Who knows where we were – the Bay of Biscay? The Galapagos Islands?

'And then suddenly they were there, out of the mist. Right in front of us. Five hundred feet away I think... St Mary's, St Agnes, Tresco. One in the north – I think it's St Margaret's. St Martin's?

'Four days and then we paddled back.'

Closer to home, other oft-repeated stories over the years feature the drug dealers who shared The Orchard for a brief period, perhaps only months. These tales also tend to get elaborated – from a bit of harmless marijuana to heavy-duty heroin dealing. However, it is true that I arrived home late one night to find the police chasing someone round The Orchard building. On another occasion, around midnight, there was a ring at the door of my flat. 'We've had an urgent message. Someone in trouble.' No point saying I was fine. They sounded serious – and genuine – so I opened the door, and two burly men flashed their badges, Starsky and Hutch style. They charged into my flat, did a recce of the place, muttered, 'sorry, false alarm,' and left.

I had a few sleepless nights and then, as quickly as they had arrived, the drug dealers were gone. The delightful Hanna replaced the heroin dealers in number seven. As she feeds her beloved squirrels at her window, she almost certainly has no idea of the former tenants of her flat.

Black George

Black George, a mile or so from The Orchard as the crow flies, stands among a cluster of inauspicious-looking cafes and bars on the main road going west towards Southall. I must have passed the pub on the 207 bus a thousand times. It's easy to miss or mistake for the Irish pub, O'Briens, further down that dismal stretch of the Uxbridge Road. Black George is tucked between the Persian Palace and a kebab shop and just along from Caspian Sandwich Bar and China Gardens. (Funny how the meanest bars and lodging houses often have the most glamorous names. I once stayed in a cockroach-infested dive – a brothel, I later realised – in Central Sumatra called Hotel Paradise.) The George is not a place for socialising, taking your girlfriend, popping in for a pint; it is for serious, under-the-table drinking. Black George is a pub of last resort. And it's where Kim, after days in a hospital ward, is heading.

Emil had phoned with the news. Kim had been given nine weeks to live. Lung cancer.

Our garden chat is now more subdued. A few of us rally round Kim, with cups of tea, as he sits forlorn in The Orchard garden. He doesn't have the heart to potter in the shed, or to put the final touches to the sign he designed to commemorate the tiny wall he had made over many

Black George

weeks to enclose a flower bed in the back garden. He had wanted to mark the occasion with reference to Donald Trump's promised wall at the Mexican border.

Three weeks pass. Kim has had a fall and is in St Mary's Hospital, Paddington. Emil, Andrzej and I share out the jobs. One of mine is to collect Kim from hospital and take him to his flat in Shepherd's Bush. Kim is in a terrible state when I arrive. Later, I realise that he has discharged himself; the nurses are concerned, but there's little they can do. He is determined to get out. He needs a drink. He's unwashed, barely clothed and stinks of urine.

Kim is not going home. He has to get his phone charged and this has to be in West Ealing. It turns out that this is where Black George is. Once outside St Mary's Hospital, I'm out of my depth. A camp young medic notices that Kim's trousers are almost round his knees, and he gives them a quick tug up with the words, 'not to worry, darling, we all have trouser problems'. Together we get Kim into a taxi, still proclaiming loudly that he has to get to West Ealing. He tells me not to worry as his mate Len is right now on a bus heading to Black George, to help get him home.

Black George. I never realised where the alcoholic and the lonely hang out during the day. It's dingy and desperate. It's Dante's *Inferno*. It's *Leaving Las Vegas*; it's the last chance saloon. I'm nervous, as a middle-class woman out of her territory: they'll think me posh. But I am welcome as Kim's friend. There is kindness and real warmth. Or maybe they are bored by the regulars. I'm a new face. They all know Kim (Emil later tells me that there are only a select number of pubs along the Uxbridge Road that Kim has not been thrown out of). And they know he has nine weeks. How the Dickens will I prise him out of the George and get him home? Finally, against the odds, Len shows up and together they start the slow pub crawl along the Uxbridge Road to the Bush and home.

Three more weeks and another fall. Kim is back on Nightingale Ward, and Andrzej and I find him in worse shape than ever. The weekend shift of 'health professionals' does not inspire confidence. Years ago, my cousin Kathleen was a nurse in Glasgow. She told me how they always gave the old boys a nip of whisky when their time was up. Not quite believing that the NHS still offers such acts of charity, I nonetheless ask the nicest young doctor around if they have any such secret supply. No luck. But she suggests I can pop out to buy him a beer at the 711 over the road. It seems a case of 'turning a blind eye' rather than positive encouragement. Andrzej, showing an unlikely compliant streak, looks very doubtful when I say I'll just pop out. 'It's

OK,' I reassure him, 'I've got permission.' Once I'm back on the ward, Kim drinks the can of Special Brew lustily, a triumphant gleam in the eye. It was probably his last beer.

Inspired by my earlier efforts for Jan, I penned an ode to Kim for the funeral at Mortlake Crematorium and added a photo of what we came to call 'Kim's wall', with the sign he had created pointing one way to Trump Tower, the second to the Mexican border.

Tribute to Kim Thorne

Kim, fondly remembered
At The Orchard, in your shed.
'Ealing born and bred,' you said,
Talented, well versed, well read.
You knew the score
And much, much more.
A clever chap, no doubt of that.
A rich, enquiring mind.
And kind.

The Orchard just won't be the same.
You went and came
Almost every day
To work or simply potter.
Well maybe not a lotta
Work was done.
But it was fun
To chew the fat
On this and that.

Kim, Kim Thorne
We'll mourn

Your passing
But remember too
The coffee over chat
At number twelve or Emil's flat.
And most of all we will recall
The sign you made to point the way
To Trump's notorious wall.

In the end, it is exactly nine weeks. Kim's friend Len comes good. He clearly functions well when sober and he's organised a decent affair at Mortlake Crematorium. Kim's only relative, a frail aunt in the West Country, is not up to the trip to Ealing, and so it is me, Emil, Len, Andrzej, Jenny the landlady at Black George and a few of the George regulars. I recognise some of them from the time I tried to lure Kim out of the pub and onto a bus back home to the Bush. Jenny says, 'He was a great storyteller.'

Kim's sign to Mexican border (site of the proposed wall) and Trump Tower

In the pub where we have the wake (not Black George but a slightly fancier one further up the Uxbridge Road on the pub crawl trail), Kim's life is set out in a few dog-eared snaps. Kim had married an Irish girl and there they are, arms entwined. Very young, no more than about eighteen. My guess is that he treated the girl badly and she left many years ago. Were there other girlfriends? Some of the Black George drinking pals talk of wives, but no one recalls a 'significant other' for Kim. I choose a black-and-white photo of Kim in seventies flared trousers. Slim then, with hair.

Some months later, it is Easter Sunday, and a rowdy bunch of very drunk guys get on the 207 bus on the Uxbridge Road. Of course they have been in Black George. These are not the polite drinkers of The Dog and Duck, nor even diners from the Persian Palace. Almost tumbling into my lap, one of the drinkers asks, 'Is that your granddaughter with you?' The young South Asian woman sitting next to me smiles, entering into the spirit of the banter.

I say, 'I bet you've been in Black George. Did you perhaps know… Kim? He was often there. Sort of sandy hair, well what was left of it. A storyteller.'

'Er no, sorry, mate.'

A wedding

It is a few weeks before Christmas 2019 and I arrive home from a long trip, jet-lagged, disorientated. Flowers everywhere. Giant tubs of foliage and lilies. Gorgeous. The usually austere corridor is transformed, the scent overwhelming.

Then I remember. While I was away – to Thailand to see my brother – James and Simone had got married in the local rugby club, just in time to share the times that lay ahead for all of us at The Orchard in 2020.

Part Two

WHACK-A-MOLE, SOMBREROS AND DROMEDARIES

Stop the surge, arrest the spike, flatten the second hump.
From speech by Boris Johnson, 17 September 2020

August 2020–September 2020

Only five months since the announcement of the Covid lockdown. It seems an eternity. Still, August and high summer bring some respite for Orchard dwellers. That is, apart from Chikayo, working round the clock, now largely on Zoom, for the Japanese School and Luca, currently doing ten-hour days in his new job in the bagel shop. But Emil is back and forth visiting his mother in Nottingham. Armando and Anna have fled for the summer to Portugal. Eszter, Tamás and their boys to Hungary. Harold and Eileen are still tucked away in Norfolk.

Cautious, I stay close to home. I never thought of myself as cautious. Now many of us are only just beginning to take tentative steps into a world where nothing is what we had supposed. Where things might never again be quite the same.

Simone and James have been bolder. The Book Bus remains out of action, while their charity work is on hold. Still, they went to the Isle of Wight on James's motorbike, Simone riding pillion – so relaxed she fell asleep. Simone is slender and light as a feather, but James describes the dead weight at his back, as she snoozed all the way to Portsmouth.

It was only a few weeks earlier in March that I wrote in my diary about how far a global event like Covid might change the way in which we interact with others, both close to home and in society at large. 'The landscape will look different', I had noted somewhat pompously.

What is new?

As the oldest of Old-Timers, I had embarked with some confidence on my ethnographic journey, charting the lives of my fellow Orchardians. But it becomes clear that I am not the all-knowing Orchard insider. Those I have called the new kids on the block, Bart and Emma in flat eleven, with their Ozzie chutzpah, outsiders, disrupters – in a good way – seem more comfortably in charge of themselves and all of us.

Will I, trapped in involuntary isolation, take to more curtain twitching and keyhole peeping? Will voyeurism become a way of life and not just a temporary aberration, a lapse of good manners in hard times? We are unsure of what boundaries are still in place, or when to break the rules. What *are* the rules? Each other's homes remain firmly out of bounds. Eszter downstairs in flat six is still washing all the vegetables, 'sanitising every item'.

Life becomes a matter of small successes, of applauding what would earlier have been modest achievements. On

17 August my diary says, 'garden lunch with Lindsay. I do gazpacho, spaghetti carbonara and smoked salmon. It is successful. We escape the rain and come indoors'. I realise that in all these months, only one other friend, Alison, has crossed my threshold, also to escape a sudden shower.

Taking the plunge

Eventually, I pluck up courage to drive short distances – down the Broadway, ten minutes to my friend Patricia in Hanwell, five minutes to the office of my solicitor, Nigel Pigeon, in Perivale. This is nothing like the grand solicitors I've occasionally been to in the City. The door is wide open, rubbish flying around – old crisp packets and abandoned face masks in the doorway. A harassed but pleasant-looking woman faces the door, almost lost in the piles of folders on her desk. A million miles away from Blake Morgan, formerly Sherwin, Son and Raper (I always preferred the old name). Gleaming steel and emptiness, not a folder anywhere. That was in the old days, pre-lockdown. Perhaps, post-lockdown, we will go local, revert to cottage industries. Nigel Pigeon's assistant is super-efficient, knows who I am, makes the copies of the legal document, an update on the lease of my flat. It is done old-fashioned style on a photocopier, and, in a matter of minutes, I stumble out into the dusty street.

For some weeks, I get no further than Perivale, until I take the plunge and, on the hottest day of the year, drive out of London in my old Nissan Micra to see my family and the alpacas. They live in a ramshackle sort of a farm, not at all what you expect of Surrey. Passing drivers stop to peer at the alpacas, but they are miserable, bad-tempered beasts. It's wise not to get too close. My niece Claire has a new baby, a beautiful, bouncy, very blond boy. His sister Chloe has gone native, running around with the chickens. 'Most of them were eaten by a fox,' she informs me gravely.

Back in Pitshanger Lane, there is some semblance of normal life. Fiona in the bookshop hides behind a Perspex screen, has disposable gloves and sanitiser at the door of her tiny shop. She recommends a Korean book that 'everyone has read in lockdown'. *Kim Jiyoung Born 1982.* I take her advice. Love it, though it is undoubtedly odd and doesn't in any clear way reflect lockdown life. Well, apart from the fact that we have perhaps become more open to new perspectives on the world. Certainly, I've never read anything quite like it. 'A groundbreaking work of feminist fiction', says one reviewer. And though it is fiction, it reads like a documentary on contemporary life for young Korean women, with cultural footnotes for the Western reader.

Having taken the feeder down from her window after the upsetting incident with the fox earlier in lockdown, Hanna, on the ground floor in number seven, now feeds the squirrels like pets. They take morsels from her outstretched hand. Mangy old squirrels have always been part of Orchard life, but now they are bushier, busier, friendlier. We see them with new eyes. Which reminds me of my friend Una who, walking one day in her village in Cambridgeshire, had a goldfinch land on her shoulder, singing its heart out. She thought it might be the basis of a magic realist novel. In fact, she was sure that the bird was her old Slovenian lover, Rolf.

A few weeks later and, though only August, it is already like autumn, the trees quite brown, conkers on the ground. Bart and Emma missed the quarantine deadline

Gentle Darius dressed for winter

coming back from France and are in lockdown for two weeks. Where is Darius? One day I see him, still, almost sculpted, profiled against a grey sky, sitting on the lawn. The original Darius was a Persian king of Babylon. Darius the dog looks regal certainly. And very silent. It can be a shock when you come across him padding up The Orchard back stairs. He's a gentle animal. Never barks but sidles up to you coyly.

Braces and red trousers

August and something is going on in The Orchard garden. Bart has put on his red trousers, braces to match, dazzling white shirt and a snazzy bow tie. He is sitting on the old green iron bench, not the fancy new one we had made in Kim's memory. Bart appears to be reading aloud the book he has written for children. *But What Are You?* tells the story of how he was adopted from Saigon, Vietnam, in

1975 and raised in Adelaide, South Australia. He arrived in a box.

The book opens:

Hi, my name is Cuong.
I was born in Vietnam during a war.
My mum and dad left me during the war so I was
sent to Australia as an orphan.
Soldiers put me in a cardboard box so I could travel
safely.
Hundreds of other babies were put into cardboard
boxes and loaded onto planes...

Bart has had a play version of the book accepted for a lockdown drama project, called Rumafest. They are rehearsing for the final film and the director, at a suitable distance – mask round his chin – stands in The Orchard garden and listens as Bart continues to recite from his book:

'When I arrived in Australia I met the Williams family. Maya Williams (Mum), Victor Williams (Dad) and Michael Williams (brother) all had light curly brown hair and blue eyes.

'I have straight black hair and brown eyes.

'"Your straight black hair is gorgeous" Mum would say every morning. Mum would smile and give me hugs all the time...'

Later this appears as a podcast. It is rather good. Bart has a strong voice and presence. He is, after all, an aspiring actor, so far mainly stunt parts but hoping for something more – he had a walk-on part in the successful TV series, *The Bodyguard*. And there's also panto at Christmas. As is common with actors, he has many strings to his bow. He is a primary school supply teacher, runs a fitness programme called Pogo Pulse, as well as supervising the daily Orchard workout sessions.

The Mail on the mat

One Sunday in late August, we strike a problem. One that leads me more than ever to doubt my judgement of my Orchard neighbours.

On the mat outside the main door is not just *The Observer* but *The Mail on Sunday*. Is this a mistake? Or is there someone in The Orchard who reads *The Mail* – not just skims through it, or reads it playfully, ironically, but orders it from the newsagent, actually *pays* for it? Should I just take it? Carefully dispose of it? God forbid, actually read it? Best perhaps leave it and spy, to find out the secret Tory reader.

I bump into Emil in the garden, washing his already immaculate Volvo. The furled umbrella ever present on the back seat, along with two hats, carefully positioned, side by side, a straw and a trilby.

'We have a serious problem at The Orchard, Emil.'

'Japanese knotweed?'

'Worse. Knotweed of the mind.'

After my outburst that Sunday morning, *The Mail on Sunday* never reappears. It crosses my mind that Emil is the mole, even as a professed man of the left – indeed a Corbynista he has claimed – and I have blown his cover as a covert Tory.

Moles, sombreros and dromedaries

Moles are suddenly everywhere. Radio 4, looking for stories of survival in hard times, notes that someone has done research on mole rats who live in the dark. Apparently, the mole rat has a highly unusual set of physical traits that allow it to thrive in a harsh underground environment. This means that they may live to 105 – not sure whether this is in human or rat years.

I decide I don't want to live till 105.

Some weeks before the doormat incident at The Orchard, Boris Johnson was also talking about moles – 'Whack-a-mole,' he said, would be a way of defeating the virus. I assumed this was a weird game that boys in elite public schools played, especially as mallets were involved, evoking croquet or polo, only played by the upper classes of England. In the event, Whack-a-Mole turns out to be the name of a fairground arcade game that involves whacking erratic plastic moles with a mallet. It seems that you stand at a waist-high cabinet, which contains a number of holes, all of which have a *mole* that pops up at random, and you're tasked with hitting it back down with the mallet.

The context for what many considered was an ill-judged metaphor was a particularly severe outbreak of Covid in one area, Leicester, of particular concern to Anna in flat five, as her mother lives in Leicester. The idea is that you knock local outbreaks 'on the head', so to speak, and other areas, even those close by, need not take any specific extra precautions. However, as one Twitter user explained at the time: 'Unless I'm mistaken, we don't have border controls between counties. Many who live in Nottingham, work in Leicester, and vice versa. Many who live in Leicester commute to London. Localised "whack-a-mole" ain't gonna cut it'. And another Twitter user added: 'Am I the only one who finds it extremely bad taste to use a gimmicky catchphrase like "whack a mole", when talking about a virus that has killed forty-five thousand people?'

Earlier, back in March, it had been sombreros, more particularly the need to 'squash the sombrero' – flatten the epidemic curve. This was the prime minister in jocular style, wanting to conjure up exotic images of Mexican mariachi musicians.

Seven months later, sombreros were abandoned in favour of dromedaries:

> *The only way to make sure the country is able to enjoy*
> *Christmas is to be tough now. So if we can grip it now,*
> *stop the surge, arrest the spike, stop the second hump of*
> *the dromedary, flatten the second hump.*
> *Dromedary or camel? I can't remember if it is a*
> *dromedary or a camel that has two humps?*
> *Anyway a double hump. So that is what we need to do!*
>
> Boris Johnson, 17 September 2020

There is a gung-ho element to all of this, as in Johnson's favourite oven-ready metaphor – just 'pop it in the oven'. Hence the famous 'oven-ready Brexit deal'.

All of this inspired me to write a mini-ode to Boris. What else can you do to let off steam when you're stuck at home?

> We've flattened the sombrero, we've turned the tide.
> Adored by the crowd, loved far and wide,
> Our cuddly Boris, blond hair askew,
> He's our hero, our darling – oven-ready, for me and for you.

Johnson is good at the Action Man narrative, socking or whacking things, wrestling with dromedaries. In early lockdown, he can just about get away with these attempts at muscular humour. Especially when it comes with a dash of supposed solidarity. Lots of 'we will put our arms around you' kind of thing.

But fancy talk cannot disguise the material reality of soaring numbers of deaths in this second surge of the virus. And only much later would we find out that Johnson had little concern about the average more or less vulnerable citizen, especially the elderly. At the official inquiry into the handling of the virus (which only gets under way in 2023), it emerges that Johnson considered deaths from Covid 'just Nature's way of dealing with old people'.

I would certainly have been one of these old folk, along with most of my friends and some fellow Orchardians, such as Harold and Eileen and, of course, my Orchard buddy, Joe O'Moricue.

Joe, as a committed socialist, is not fooled by Johnson's rhetoric – even at a time when it is playing pretty well to the rest of the country: 'Things could hardly be worse,' he says one day when I come across him in the Arboretum. 'If this was a Labour government, they'd be talking about bringing in the military.'

I'm ready to join in: 'One problem is that the Tories are good at putting a positive spin on even the worst of circumstances, with the talk not just of jokey things like dromedaries but road maps and circuit breakers. They tell a good story.'

Joe warms to this theme. 'The right wing have got all the best songs. They've got prejudice, sneakiness, meanness. People love that kind of thing.'

The bad ethnographer

Over the next few months, further clues indicate my inadequacy as The Orchard's ethnographer. A bottle of real champagne – not the ubiquitous Prosecco – is left outside James and Simone's door on the first-floor corridor. A special birthday? Or is it their wedding anniversary? Could it be that a whole year has gone by since I flew in jet-lagged that morning and The Orchard was full of lilies?

No, of course not. It is barely six months. But that was in the world Before Lockdown.

BUBBLES, ZOOMING AND HAIKUS

A bubble is a group of people with whom you have close physical contact. Bubbles must be 'exclusive'. Once in one, you can't start another with a different household. If you decide to change your bubble, you should treat your previous bubble as a separate household for ten days before forming a new one.

Government guidelines, 6 January 2021

September 2020

Lockdown has brought to The Orchard new alliances, new ways of looking at the world, but also new language. One word is 'bubbles'.

Bubbles entered our lives a bit later than some of the earlier, more aggressive metaphors to characterise the Covid experience, like 'whack-a-mole' and things that 'surged' and 'spiked'. In those early lockdown days, the virus was described as an 'enemy' to be 'beaten', a 'tsunami'. Unlike counsels to fight, to resist, to stand firm, 'bubbles' shifts the narrative, suggesting protection, cosiness, keeping safe. Bubbles is a comfy-sounding word from childhood, as in 'blowing bubbles'.

I had an idea that only people like grannies could be 'in a bubble'. The closest I come to this is as Great Aunt, which doesn't really count.

Grannies got a lot of media attention in early lockdown, along with talk about 'missing hugs' from grandchildren – even though I couldn't resist the thought that, as many of this older generation had wrecked the futures of children and grandchildren by voting for Brexit, the kids themselves might not be so keen on such familial embraces.

The bubble-less

'Bubble-less' sounds sad. A bit like 'friendless'. *Are Joe and I in a bubble?* we ponder. Not together, that is, with each other – we are not that close – but if not, then with *whom*? And yes, we have family, some of whom we are fond of and they of us, but they are miles away. Consequently, Joe and I are hungry for talk – always at a distance of course – when our paths cross on the daily perambulations.

On this particular day, I catch Joe coming out of number eight. Really slimmed down, a sexy beard and longish but well-groomed hair. Fancy braces too. He's now working two days a week. Painting and decorating job in Hanwell, he says. Lockdown has been good for him. Before he looked a bit down and out – now he's glamorously bohemian.

Joe and I barely talked before. Alone and bubble-less, we have become lockdown buddies. We jabber away – find out things we never knew about each other. We share a northern background. I tell Joe that I was brought up in Leigh, which was then in Lancashire, now in Greater Manchester – 5 Churchill Avenue, parallel with Attlee

Avenue, right next to Eden Drive and Bevin Close, still there on Google Maps. Formerly social housing, now, one supposes, post-Thatcher, privately owned. Leigh is constantly in the news as one of the 'blue wall' seats – former Labour strongholds who have rallied to Johnson's Brexit call; folk saying how their lifelong Labour-supporting fathers, mothers, grandparents 'would turn in their graves' at the thought of their children and grandchildren voting Tory. There must be a lot of disturbed graves in Leigh.

Joe says that his father was a miner in that area. Both his mother and father came from Ireland. His mother was in service. He talks about the fifties and sixties and then how, in 1972, he went to Australia, came back to Britain twenty years later and found that things were better. Not so much cap doffing.

I'm surprised to learn he's been at The Orchard for ten years.

Joe: 'I've been here ten years, since I split with my missus. I was married for thirty years, together for thirty-five years. Born in Manchester, Irish Catholic family. Basically lived in Australia for twenty-odd years. Mostly in the building game and painting.'

Cathie: 'So you left school and then you went straight to work?'

J: 'Straight to work at fifteen. I was an indentured painter and decorator. On the indentures when you signed them, you actually gave the master the right – you had to ask him for permission to get married. You was indentured till the age of twenty-one, so he became the guardian in a sense. Harkening back to medieval times!'

C: 'So did you have to *ask* him when you got married?'

J: 'Oh no, no, no.'

C: 'You weren't that young?'

J: 'What I'm saying is that it shows how things have changed.'

Who is most working class?

Once Joe and I get into our stride, we are prone to indulge in 'who is the most working class?' kind of competitive talk. It is reminiscent of the famous Monty Python sketch, which features four guys boasting about how each has more proletarian roots than his fellow.

C: 'It's another world… I can remember the sound of clogs on cobbled streets. If I said that to my nieces and nephew, they would roar with laughter, but I *have* got that memory.'

J: 'Me too. I lived in Oldham near Manchester. Still mills in Oldham when I was young. And I can still remember people using lip-reading on the bus, because they were used to lip-reading in the factory – with all the noise.

'I used to see people who had rickets. Cos rickets in the twenties and thirties were terrible – you'd see old people full of rickets.'

C: 'My father's family lived in Greenock in Western Scotland. So when we got enough money to get a car, we'd drive the old Ford Prefect to Scotland to see the family, and I remember we'd be driving through the Gorbals in Glasgow. Late in the evening by then. It took fourteen hours to make that journey (from the South of England) in those days.

'What I remember is how short the men were, with their flat caps, standing on street corners round slum buildings. Just standing there. I always remember that.'

J: 'Look at me. My stature. I come from that same sort of background.'

C: 'How many brothers and sisters did you have?'

J: 'There were seven of us. Five boys and two girls.'

C: 'Were you close growing up?'

J: 'Oh yes. Still are. We still all communicate. And still carry on. This brother now, in Manchester, he's the eldest. He's not well, but touch wood… he's kept going. He's kept going through Covid. He was on palliative care at Christmas. They gave him six weeks to live.

'Two brothers in Australia. Another brother up in Manchester. Two sisters in Manchester.'

C: 'My father was one of seven.'

J: 'Seven wasn't big. Eleven or twelve was average.'

C: 'Three died prematurely so there were only four.'

J: 'I think my mum lost a couple in miscarriages.'

Joe and I also indulge in what the artist and social commentator Grayson Perry recently called the typically English trait of 'nostalgia for bad times'.

C: 'I remember being freezing cold. We lived in a prefab for a time, and they were freezing cold. Frost on the windows every morning.'

J: 'Lino on the floor.'

C: 'I'm not saying we were poor, poor, poor. We weren't well off but when you're growing up you don't feel it – you don't think, *this is awful*.'

J: 'Everybody on the street is the same. A guy growing up in a mud hut in Africa don't feel it, till he goes to the town. I think it was more of a blessing to see that side of life.

'Now it's just – what's the word for it? Bland – there's a blandness about modernity.

'I enjoy seeing ugly people. You don't see ugly people anymore. No characters anymore. Everyone's got good hair. Cathie, you must have grown up with buck teeth, people with teeth missing, bow legged. It was more... you did actually see ugly people – I mean ugly in the sense... I mean not ugly as *people*, not as *human beings*, but like a lip was over here and...

'Once you take the grit out of it – don't get me wrong – it's looking at it with rose-coloured glasses. We didn't like it at the time, did we? But – I've said this often – I don't envy being young. You'd never think an old person would say that. It was smoky and gritty. I miss it.'

Fans and Zooming

Joe and I are taking a bit of a risk in our spoken encounters when we bump into each other on the daily walk, or as we pause on The Orchard garden seat: talking – especially loudly – means spreading those droplets. Today a woman, having joined the daily circuit of walkers and joggers around Hanger Hill Park, going north from The Orchard, was barking her head off. She hadn't lost it in lockdown but was merely speaking on the phone, very loudly, in Italian. In multilingual Ealing, we eavesdroppers are used to picking up snatches of Spanish, Italian, Polish, Japanese or Arabic. People living in small flats need to let off steam out of doors, make crucial work calls or conduct affairs behind the backs of their lockdown companions.

To replace talk, my friend Jennifer continues to promote the idea of fans. She explains that there is a whole language of fans. I point out that fans would just spread the germs around. But no, she means using a fan coquettishly, holding it close to one's body.

'We do it all with our eyes like the old courtesans. No speaking – so no spreading of germs that way,' says Jennifer triumphantly.

And of course, Zoom has come to replace face-to-face communication among friendship groups, families and students at university. With this comes a new language of chat, muting and unmuting. And just when we get to grips, sort of, with Zoom, we have Teams and then Blackboard and, God help us, 'breakthrough rooms'– or is it 'breakout'? Lately, a new one, something called 'hovering'. Just 'hover' over it, I'm told. 'Over what?' I mutter. And of course, all over the land, people are shrieking, 'you've frozen!' or, 'unmute!'

Pre-lockdown, our reading group – Bookbreak we call it – met every Wednesday in Ladbroke Grove Library. Though there are regulars who have attended for some years, it's also the sort of group where people drop by. Everyone is welcome – the lonely, the depressed, or those who just love reading – reading aloud. We come together as near-strangers, knowing little of our fellow readers, beyond the couple of hours spent in each other's company. A line of poetry or a moment in a novel may trigger a confidence, a personal anecdote. But these are always spontaneously offered, never sought. Now a few of us in the original group have migrated to Zoom for our weekly read-alongs. Distance, in some ways, brings us closer, as we see people at home, speculate on their taste in decorating, the choice of prints on the wall, the kind of clutter they feel comfortable with. Group leader Ian's laptop is set up in his kitchen, and I become fixated by the clock on the wall, just above his handsome head, which keeps sinking, as Ian is as inept with the technology as I am. We spend a lot of time addressing his eyebrows. Over this year, I have seen Ian more often than my closest friends. Still, there are boundaries that will not be crossed. I will never enter that kitchen. We are Zoom buddies, suspended in a particular space.

And Zoom has replaced the annual AGM at The Orchard, which normally takes place in Andrzej and Ewa's handsome living room, full of heirlooms, carefully framed family photos displayed on the grandest of grand pianos. Now we Orchard folk are scattered, mainly in London but some further afield: there are Harold and Eileen, peering at us from far away Norfolk. The normally sleek Harold with surprisingly wild hair; James, with even longer hair, still looking like a not-even-aging rock star. Andrzej, as his screen backdrop, has two swords in scabbards, of the kind you see on the walls of stately homes. Testimony perhaps to aristocratic connections. I realise – too late – that my own Zoom background is the old ironing board, propped up against the wall of my study.

Later Emil tells me, when I check on the aristocratic connotations, that Andrzej's father was the last Postmaster General in 1930s Poland. A very important honorary position. 'Why the last?'

'Someone called Hitler turned up', is Emil's laconic reply.

Of course, Zoom simply doesn't work in many situations. Not just older folk who cannot get to grips with it, like my friend Jennifer, but workers such as those in transport or retail and cleaning staff whose job depends on being physically present. You cannot clean a room virtually.

It follows that, in all these months, my cleaner Brzoska has made only an occasional appearance at number twelve.

And even when some regularity is resumed, talk is highly constrained: when she arrives, I nip out; we write notes for one another. Brzoska – whose written English has never quite caught up with her excellent spoken English – leaves notes all over the flat, a bit like her Marigold gloves, which also turn up in odd places, like in the oven, in pot plants, on the mantelpiece.

She brings Polish delicacies.

In Freage you find sussages. I hope you like it.

Brzoska's terseness is now common. The early lockdown days of long emails and expansiveness have collapsed into brief messages and minimalist exchanges. Sarah, my old friend from Questors Theatre who lives just round the corner from The Orchard, has broken her arm and emails from Hillingdon Hospital.

Y phone quite dead as have no charger with me. Have been back in HILLINGDON FOR OP ON ELBOW ANDARM NOWI PLASTERWHI H MUST COME ODF AS ITISEXCRUTIATING. HOOPING TO BE MOVED TO CLAYPONDSAGAIN. CIF THEy accept me. '. Cannot typewith left handi am so clumsy. Eenwwashedsoamclea atlest. Sarah. Xxx

And a few days later:

Hi Insist on sending. Me home say I am a tough. Old bird. Not at all sure I can cope and am. Very very anxious especially about night time and getting off toilet asssumjing I can get on it. Claypondsdo not seem to want me. If I am home please end see me.xxxxx Sent from my iPad

Haikus

Haikus, introduced to me by Chikayo, our lovely Orchard neighbour in flat twenty, seem a perfect minimal communication tool for lockdown times. A haiku is an unrhymed Japanese poetic form that consists of seventeen syllables, arranged in three lines containing five, seven and five syllables, respectively. Originally hymns to natural beauty, with depth of feeling, in lockdown haikus have been adopted for new causes, especially of offer and thanks. One in the Co-op in the Lane, provided (I think) by a satisfied customer, is pinned up on a scrappy bit of paper. It reads:

A Haiku for the Co-op

The Co-op is great
Go forward in leaps and bounds
Outstrip the rest

(Though I make the last line only four syllables.)

Harold and Eileen have made a quick foray to Ealing from Norfolk. I miss them but stumble across a bag of apples outside my back door. They send an email:

Have left you a few apples from our garden on your back doorstep. They're Norfolk Royal Russets – not very much like normal russets and not very royal. So OK for republican consumption, we think.

With a bit of tweaking, this becomes a seventeen-syllable haiku:

Have left some apples:
'Royal Russets' – *not* royal
So perfect for you.

To which my reply is:

> Warm thanks for the gift:
> Apples. Left on the doorstep:
> Royal Russets. So kind.

A GOOD DEED IN A NAUGHTY WORLD

'Warmest thanks to you two
Who've helped me get through
This horrible year
With barely a tear'

From 'Song of the Champagne Socialist', by Cathie Wallace

September 2020-December 2020

Exactly six months since my personal lockdown on 17 March. Since I started my diary.

Children rush along Montpelier Road on their way to school, excited by the novelty, after weeks of home tuition, followed by the summer holiday. Scooters, cars, bikes. The peace of the earlier days has vanished. Among the melee, I spot Arin from number eighteen in smart new glasses.

In the wasteland next door, earmarked for a fancy house by a local property developer, the foxes have completely taken over. Our vixen has bred prodigiously and her cubs, growing fast, are having a whale of a time.

A scarlet house plant – a poinsettia – gleams from James and Simone's window. Mindful of my neighbours' kindness during the lockdown months, I think of Portia's line in *The Merchant of Venice*:

> *That light we see is burning in my hall*
> *How far that little candle throws his beams!*
> *So shines a good deed in a naughty world.*
> *The Merchant of Venice*, Act 5, Scene 1, William Shakespeare

Hanging out

On a lovely September morning, I see everyone hanging out, either in the garden or in the corridor on the first floor.

My next-door neighbour, Bart, is doing handstands in the garden, taking advantage of glorious autumn sunshine.

Emil stands outside his flat, working on his laptop, while Brzoska – who is now also 'doing' for Emil – cleans within. His extensive library is piled up in the corridor. Brzoska tells me that his flat is filled with books, pretty much taking up all the floor space, as a spillover from shelves on every wall. He has to turf the books out into the corridor so she can do the hoovering. I turn my head sideways to read the titles. Many are first editions of authors such as Vladimir Nabokov and J.G. Ballard.

The survey of Emil's books piled in the corridor leads me to take another look at my own, less impressive, collection. Prominent is Noel's copy of Shakespeare – the one I gave him for his sixtieth birthday and that often props up my iPad – a use of a treasured gift that feels disrespectful to Noel's memory. Nestling next to *The Riverside Shakespeare* is *Electricity, Its Theory, Sources and Applications*. This hefty tome was written by my great-great-grandfather and, so says the blurb, considered 'part

Emily's bookcase at number Fourteen

of the knowledge base of civilization as we know it', no less.

John T. Sprague deserves his place on the bookshelf, as my only relative of note. A few years ago, I idly googled his name, and his book popped up, available through Amazon. It seems that a digital copy was preserved for generations on library shelves before it was scanned by Google as part of a project to make the world's books discoverable online. It has survived long enough for the copyright to expire and the book to enter the public domain. Public domain books are, Google tells us, 'our gateways to the past, representing a wealth of history, culture and knowledge that's often difficult to discover'.

A copy of the book – costing £20 – arrives the next day.

While *Electricity* and *The Riverside Shakespeare* are unlikely companions, elsewhere there is method in the madness. Noel's books (those he wrote, such as *Playwriting and Young People, New Theatre* and – my favourite, a collection of plays for children – *Tin Soldier*) sit side by

Noel's bookcase

side with his favourite texts, not just the Shakespeare but *A Summer Book* and *A Winter Book* by Tove Jansson, Steinbeck's *The Grapes of Wrath* and John Berger's *Ways of Seeing*.

Facing Noel's bookcase is my mother's bookcase. More homely titles, as well as lots of Trollope, whom she loved. Kim made both of these bookcases specially to fit this space in my living room and didn't do a bad job. There are always loose ends and rough edges with his craftsmanship, but also things done lovingly, such as the eccentric art deco-inspired fireplace in Emil's living room.

During lockdown, books have become cultural currency. More than ever, you are judged by what is on display. Especially in Zoom shots, we sum people up by their personal library choices; volumes, preferably hardbacked, are sometimes piled on bookshelves higgledy-piggledy, sometimes arranged in a highly self-conscious way, the result of careful curating. Tory politicians play safe with David Attenborough or Boris Johnson's biography of Churchill. Braver or leftier ones have Piketty's *Capital* or

Brett Christopher's *Rentier Capitalism* or *Why We Can't Afford the Rich* by Andrew Sayer. The then Prince Charles – now King – faces the camera in front of a library with ancient volumes encased within glass-fronted bookcases, never opened, one imagines. One journalist, a regular on one of my favourite news programmes, ensures that the writing on a mug on his desk is just visible. It says 'I STILL HATE THATCHER'.

On this particular morning, out the front, Joe is loading his car. Help! Is he leaving? Joe told me once that he's been poised to leave The Orchard pretty much since he arrived. Boxes still unpacked, he says. Back to Australia perhaps? But no, he's just going to Manchester, where his brother is ill. Knowing how much he loves to draw trees, I tell him about the beautiful lime tree in the Arboretum. But, as I'd guessed, this is too pretty for Joe. He does 'gnarled'. Or simply 'ordinary'. There's a tree in Lammas Park, unexceptional but special to him. A sycamore. That's the one he's drawing. In Mattock Lane, he says, near the pond with the ducks.

Stephanie and Rob from flat fifteen turn up too, laden with loo rolls. Preparing for a harder lockdown.

Stephanie now has a job with Ealing Council in local health, as she had said a few days earlier when we met in the park. We had admired the small display of wild flowers in the Arboretum, maybe planted, thought Emil, by the schoolchildren next door in Montpelier School.

Inspired by the impressive display in the park, I order seeds from Friends of the Earth. Bee attracting. This reminds me of Valentina and her phobia about bees. I haven't seen her for weeks, though I guess she is still hunkered down in flat three with her two handsome men.

Then suddenly there they are, Valentina and Luca round the corner, smoking – furtively since Emil's reprimand back in May. They approach, not too close, accosting me with touching warmth.

'We were just talking about you – we haven't seen you for ages!'

We speak English and, in truth, my Italian is now very rusty. No practice for months. Another lost lockdown opportunity – we're supposed to at least brush up the languages we know, preferably learn new ones, like Swahili. I had tried Korean a few years ago, on the grounds that it has a fascinating, unique writing system, known as Hangul. Koreans are proud of their script, invented by a popular king who designed the new alphabet so that even those with little education could learn to read and write: 'A wise man can acquaint himself with [the script] before the morning is over; a stupid man can learn it in the space of ten days,' said Sejong the Great. I must be stupid indeed, as I never got to grips with even the basics of either written or spoken Korean.

Luca and Valentina say they're fine. Lorenzo has started at the local Catholic primary school, St Gregory's. The other three Orchard boys go to Montpelier, where for years a favourite teacher went by the wonderful name of Rusty McAdam. Rusty was legendary, loved by generations of children and their parents. Refused to be headteacher but so popular they named one of the school buildings after him. No one else has had such honour bestowed on them.

That same evening it's garden drinks. The nights are closing in. At a certain point, the vixen passes through to check out her territory, coming through the hole in the bottom of the fence from her domain next door. Emil comes with his mum, Barbara. A charming woman who was born in Lebanon and moved to Russia as a young woman, before marriage and life in Nottingham. A cosmopolitan story. Bart and Emma show up with Darius. This is when I learn that Darius is not just a celebrity dog but is a therapy dog, available for hire to old people's homes, or to those suffering from depression or anxiety. And Darius has had therapy too, dog therapy. Like human therapists, dogs have to share the experience of their clients. Darius is also registered with the animal talent agency Urban Paws, which tells us:

> *Darius has an aristocratic bearing with a relaxed temperament making him ideal for specific roles, according to his dog skill set.*

He can 'howl on command' and 'ride on a surfboard', this skill not terribly useful in urban Ealing, reminding us that Darius is at heart an Aussie dog, at home on Bondi Beach rather than down the Broadway.

Everyone tells stories. Simone embarks on what I think is the start of her love affair with James, but we don't get beyond the elephants in the bush in Botswana. They had closed camp for the night, they thought, but had left one onion on the table. The elephants will pursue any kind of food, by smell, to the end. They don't mean harm, but they persist. So the beautiful china, which Simone had insisted on bringing with them, was destroyed. Everything trashed.

But we never get to the end of the story. It might have been at this point that the vixen passed through, checking us out. I think she occasionally leaves poo right by Kim's bench, just to let us know who's boss.

Groundhog Day

As we move into autumn, my diary features many entries of the kind like the following: 'where did the day go? No writing, a little reading and emailing. I make leek and potato soup. Again.'

Not just the day: where did the *weeks* go? We tried half-heartedly to plan ahead, to hold to some sense of purpose. James and I planted the seeds sent by Friends of the Earth. They might come up by next spring. And two delightful shrubs face Hanna's window on the ground floor. The orange flowers have faded but the white still shine. The leaves are quite brown now and have mainly fallen.

James and Simone have just discovered the iconic film *Groundhog Day*. They are watching it – again and again of course. Each day the same: the struggle to bring some sense of moving forward. Right now, the end is not in sight; the days are eerily similar.

My routine doesn't change. I switch on the radio, stagger downstairs to get *The Guardian*, slipped under the mat in the hall on the ground floor, hoping now not to bump into folk as my hair looks wilder than ever. I missed the last hairdressing slot with Larry, the only hairdresser I trust with my hair. I feel disloyal if I try another stylist.

Larry. We have grown old together. He must have been a lad of sixteen when he first cut my hair, recommended I think by a boyfriend of that time. Mine not Larry's. Larry is married to Alice, no children. He hates children, he said once, rather unexpectedly for so mild a man. He often talks of going for a drink at the Conservative Club. That's another change – there used to be a large blue sign just on that roundabout coming into Ealing from Brentford, that stretch of the road where the beautiful old chestnuts stand. But the Con Club, as my mum always called it, no longer proclaims its identity in lefty-leaning Ealing.

My life is measured out, not in spoons but shopping lists. Another Monday. Time for James's weekly trip in The Book Bus to Waitrose to get Orchard provisions. I try to do the shopping list in rhyme, to ring the changes:

Song of the Champagne Socialist
A packet of loose Waitrose tea,
Wine – Cava for you and Claret for me –
Steaks, two salmon, one beef,
Tea – not teabags but leaf –
Damn it, I've already put that.
Milk, semi-skimmed not full fat,
Bran flakes, cream and brown sugar
And, oh bugger
– I almost forgot –
In a pack, not a pot,
That delicious cream cheese.
Veg – beans, leeks or peas –
Coffee of course, and loo rolls –
Plenty of those,
That's of course if the shelves are not bare.
Nothing to do then but weep in despair.

Later I add a stanza when I deliver this tribute to James and Simone at Christmas:

So warmest thanks to you two,
Who've helped me get through
This horrible year
With barely a tear.

Serial killers and 'Dancing Queen'

October arrives. I write in my diary on 15 October: 'just seven months after the initial lockdown, there is no longer any mixing of households indoors. And it's bad news for Ealing. It is all over the airwaves that we are the "worst affected in London", especially Southall, it seems'.

Our school governor meeting on Zoom is also depressing. The school is in a disadvantaged part of Ealing, in the northern reaches of the borough. More than ever are staff, from necessity as well as dedication, acting as social workers, doing everything, not just for the kids but their parents too. Teachers who are known and trusted by the families take to going round to homes, knocking on doors, keeping their distance on the doorstep. The register is taken online, and if the children don't make some kind of virtual appearance, off goes a stalwart staff member to lure the children out of their pyjamas, into school uniform and in front of the screens.

Renewed isolation means even more time indoors. People have been resourceful in lockdown. Cooking and baking of course – mountains of sourdough and banana bread. Walking. Joe, fitter than he's been in years, after covering pretty much the whole of the borough on his morning hikes. Painting if they can – or even if they can't. My friend Phillipa has done a terrifying self-portrait; a portrait of her partner Adrian slightly less so.

Steve McQueen's *Small Axe* on TV is a treat. *The Crown*

of course. Time to binge on the *Line of Duty* episodes you missed, now so complicated that older, less agile brains have to watch each episode at least twice. That takes care of a bit of time.

Now we have all the time in the world. No trains or buses to catch, certainly no planes. After years of rushing around, I'm going nowhere – well, just round the park and back home. I may sit for hours searching for the little vixen, spotting the two jays who are certainly mates and building a nest in the old yew tree.

Doorstep gifts continue to arrive, though the flow has slightly dried up. More apples from Norfolk, herbs from Provence, whither Chikayo sneaked off on a brief visit. One day a wonderful piece of birthday cake, as it's Emil's fifty-fourth birthday. Not as good as Simone's home baking but glorious technicolour.

Lockdown has triggered messages from old friends, some not heard from in years. Michela in Genoa, always a wonderful linguist, now, with time on her hands, adding Serbo-Croat to her repertoire. My friend Camille in France is reading *Middlemarch* to her lover. As Marie-Claude is stranded in Paris, this has to be over the phone – in English thankfully. But still, this is a stretch. There is a sense that now is the time to read *Ulysses*, *War and Peace* and as much of Dickens as possible. Una opted for *La Peste* in the original French and Camille is writing the definitive biography of Proust, out there in her isolated village in the Hautes-Alpes.

Closer to home in Hanwell, Patricia will only listen to ABBA and, when she's feeling low, rehearses her moves to 'Dancing Queen'. I haven't the heart to tell her that Dominic Cummings was supposedly observed bopping to the same tune, in the middle of the first wave of the virus infection, up in his family estate in Durham. Patricia likes the feel-good stuff, as do many of us in lockdown, and avoids all the serial killers, so I feel guilty after recommending what I thought might be a cosy Scandi noir for the long, lonely winter evenings. It had turned out to be unusually bloody.

Round the back at The Orchard, Emil finds me clearing the drains and makes an inappropriate joke about Dennis Nilsen. He has also been watching all the TV programmes on serial killers.

The serial killers continue. One last night about the notorious doctor Harold Shipman, who killed an alarming number of his patients, had me wondering. Very *Arsenic and Old Lace* (well, in reverse I suppose, as in that film classic, the old ladies did the killing, as I recall). Or *Ladykillers*, a famous Ealing comedy. We did it at Questors and I had a walk-on part. In the play, Mrs Wilberforce turns the tables and each of the original ladykillers meets a grisly end. The old lady escapes, triumphant.

Not so, sadly, with Shipman's victims. The TV series is done respectfully. But I have questions: if the old ladies – about my age, I realise – were perfectly healthy, which there is reason to suppose many were, how did Shipman just arrive on their doorstep, syringe in hand? I am mystified. I somehow cannot imagine this of my GP, Dr McWhinney, Irish and laconic. A man of few words. 'Ah, Miss Wallace, I've just dropped round to check your blood pressure', before then popping the morphine-filled syringe into my arm.

A rose in November

November and we are back to pretty well total lockdown. Only the schools might be saved from closure and now even this is in question.

The garden is sad. The Prosecco parties abandoned. But suddenly, a startlingly red rose blooms in the pot a friend gave me for my birthday. This may be the work of our nurturing gardener, Laurie – not the two slash-and-burn guys. I am becoming aware that Laurie is a resurrected Kim, Andrzej's stooge, a new double act. They are busy setting up the same tetchy, half-humorous relationship. 'Always fixing up his fleet of Porsches– parked in everyone's way out the back,' mutters Laurie.

Luca scuttles by. No lingering or chatting now, just a quick enough exchange for him to say he is still looking for work. It will be hard. But he is thinking of a delivery job. That could work; there's lots of jobs there now that people are avoiding face-to-face shopping, perhaps at the online business I eventually managed to access. Zoom by Ocado only operates in the leafier parts of West London – so very champagne socialist. I suspect exploitation, as young people arrive with the booty, often with minimal English, usually on motorbikes. Some of the couriers are the Brazilians I came across a few weeks earlier, hanging out on the green in central Ealing, during the first hiatus from Covid. I am now in the odd position that James and Simone shop for me while I shop online for Patricia. I pop the stuff round to Hanwell and leave it on the doorstep. But it makes some kind of sense. I want to avoid Patricia nipping out to get dog food for her pet spaniel, Honey. The problem is that Zoom by Ocado has run out of dog food. They've also fallen victim to the curse of The Orchard. No street number. The couriers are sent to the far corners of the borough. I get frantic phone calls. Often, they say, 'I'm at the roundabout.' But which one? I run around the local streets, eventually piloting them back to the elusive Orchard block.

And it is around this time I discover that there is a whole other life that has eluded me at The Orchard. This appears to go on behind the garages. I have not done the duty of an anthropologist after all. I have missed a key scene of socialising. This is where the interesting conversations and developing friendships are taking place. This is where Joe keeps his canvasses. A special shed, no less. And Joe is giving Emma drawing lessons. I'm not sure how this can be managed at a distance. Whatever the case, I find myself oddly jealous. How could I not have known? I discover too that Hanna and her chap Ziggy do interesting things in their garage. I think it is something athletic.

A Serbian spruce

By early December, we are still hoping for some kind of Christmas. We dare to make plans. James and Simone to Ireland for a large family gathering. Joe to his brother and niece in Manchester. For me a smallish get-together on the South Coast, but nonetheless we're planning for the usual ten to twelve people.

For a while it stays that way. I have been enlisted to ensure the children have a good time. We need some innovative games – which have to be non-contact of course. I pick up advice from the indispensable Radio 4. 'The best way to stay safe is to imagine that one of you is infected.' 'Which one of you is infected?' is surely a party game that will bring Christmas cheer. How would this work? Perhaps we all mimic symptoms: a version of charades in which you express extreme fatigue, brain fog, a hacking cough. The best actor is the winner. I put this idea to my niece, who is hosting Christmas. It doesn't go down well.

Mid-December and another last-minute turnaround from Boris Johnson. We in London and the South East – so we are now informed – are in Tier Four. Tiers now seem a lifetime ago but were Covid currency at the time. This means that no one is going anywhere. Christmas will be here at The Orchard. To cheer us up, James has organised an Orchard Christmas tree, something we haven't bothered with before. He announces the plan in a round robin email, haiku style:

A Christmas tree for the porch.
Will send pictures once it's in place.
A Serbian Spruce!

A few days later and James has put up the Serbian spruce in the entrance. The idea is that the four boys in the block will decorate it. That is, the two Hungarian boys, Arin from number eighteen upstairs and Lorenzo, the elusive Italian lad in flat three, he who nurtured the garden seedlings in summer. I suspect the adults have got there first. Each day someone has tweaked the decorations, added a bauble, rearranged a bit of sparkly stuff.

Today, eight days before Christmas, the adult tree has given birth. There is a baby Christmas tree on the little shelf next to its parent.

Over the road from The Orchard, there is the annual dazzling display of Christmas lights on one of the more imposing houses in Montpelier Road. My cab-driving friends tell me that the owner of the house is a very generous Indian woman, wealthy enough to fund the spectacle. Cars stop, families gawp, many making a special journey. Some sneer. But most of us cheer. Reindeer, sleighs, elves, gnomes reappear each December, gloriously unchanged, like the figures on Keats' 'Grecian Urn'. This year, however, the lighting has faltered, and instead of the intended joyous raising of both arms, only the right arm of Father Christmas is lit in the upward option. He appears to be doing a Heil Hitler salute.

Blinking in the hectic illumination from the house across the street, ablaze with lights, some of us have risked a social gathering, huddling under The Orchard canopy over the front door. It is a week before Christmas. Bart and Emma have brought the inevitable Prosecco; I've got the stollen and mince pies. And I've found a bottle of mulled wine at the back of the pantry, given to me by my niece Claire years ago in a hamper she probably got cheap. While we are still largely compliant, there is defiance too – and indulgence. It's been a hard year. We deserve to eat and drink a little more than we should; my niece Kate cracked open a gift-wrapped panettone, all set to go off to her mother-in-law in Dumfries. I attacked a rich stollen, sitting temptingly on my kitchen counter.

The Friday before Christmas Emma and Bart and Darius the dog knock at the back door. Unabashed in their Ozzie good humour, they hand over a bottle of Prosecco. Even Darius has a Father Christmas hat on and Emma a wonderful satin Santa jacket.

On Christmas Eve, the Hungarian boys Gergő and Balint come to my door. They stand like silent carol singers, masked, each holding out a small, beautifully wrapped candle and a Christmas card.

The day itself. No family visiting and a million Zoom calls across the land.

CORRIDORS OF UNCERTAINTY

Whether an oppressive tool of state power or unsettling locus of supernatural disquiet, the corridor has come to embody a unique form of experiential desolation.

From 'Corridors of uncertainty: Modernist utopia and cinematic menace' (Catherine Slessor, 2020)

From Christmas 2020

Saturday nights on The Orchard first-floor corridor began after the Christmas dinner in 2020, when, desperate for sociability, we settled on this space, as 'not quite indoors'. In truth, the dinner had been a lacklustre affair. The attempt at festivity was a struggle. The Father Christmas outfits, masks to match. Darius, the handsome Hungarian pointer, also in Christmas regalia. Nothing helped much. But we were hungry, not for my overcooked parsnips, not even for Simone and James's turkey crown, but for connectedness.

The irrepressible Bart and Emma had insisted on some kind of Christmas. After all, no one could go anywhere. We were marooned. The corridor was the compromise option.

Nervously, I agreed to take part. I retreated early, but the carousing continued till late into the night. We'd been cooped up for so long that a couple of glasses of champagne threw caution to the winds. I was nervous. All those potentially lethal droplets flying about and landing who knows where.

Limbo

'Corridor' does not conjure up anything pleasant. Comparable words describing confined or long and narrow spaces include 'landing', 'hallway', as well as liturgical, even romantic or poetic names, such as 'cloister' and 'aisle'. 'Corridor' suggests stark functionality, a public thoroughfare, a convenience. The quickest route from one place to another, not important in itself. There is a sense of provisionality, of uncertainty, of being in limbo. But also things hidden, in the dark, the never-to-be-known lives of people behind closed doors. There is at least one horror

The first-floor corridor

film that draws on the word: *Corridors of Blood*, starring Boris Karloff and Christopher Lee. Later came classics such as *The Shining*, showing corridors with rooms off them. Or stairs going who knows where?

In her paper on corridors, architect Catherine Slessor expands on the theme:

> In Charlotte Brontë's Jane Eyre, *the first Mrs Rochester vengefully roams the corridors of Thornfield Hall after dark, seeking retribution. And in innumerable detective novels set in grand hotels, bourgeois residents are perpetually in peril, as Walter Benjamin observes, 'tremulously awaiting the nameless murderer', who skulks in corridors and lobbies.*

Catherine Slessor, 2020

Even when used metaphorically, connotations are negative, as in 'corridors of power', summoning up notions of covert influence, things sinister, illicit.

And my corridor – the one on the first floor – is no exception. It brings to mind the words of Catherine Slessor: 'experiential desolation'. Drab anonymity, shading into menace. It was the sense of threat that had attracted the site director for the episode of *Morse*, 'Driven to Distraction'. The corridor was itself a major character in what the website calls DtoD. Feet echoing along the unlit Orchard corridor. Bars added to the small window in the front door of flat eleven, which made the character of Phillipa Lao seem more helpless and vulnerable, as she is seen answering the insistent ringing of a doorbell. Featuring a deranged driving instructor, who doubles up as a serial killer, this episode – even through written by the much-admired Anthony Minghella – attracted blistering reviews:

> *The most clichéd, cheap and fear mongering sort of film making... the stuff of second rate slasher cheapies.*
>
> User review

As it happens, we are talking not just of fictional murders in this part of leafy Ealing, but real murders. Well, not actually *in* The Orchard, but as near as dammit. In July 1988, just a year before the *Morse* filming, there was a dramatic, never-solved murder in a block of flats more or less on our doorstep. It came to be known as 'the crossbow murder', taking place right outside the poor woman's front door. In her corridor.

Over the years, we tried to make The Orchard corridors cosier. The carpet from the drab hotel in Shepherd's Bush replaced the atmospheric linoleum that had worked so well in *Morse*. On the top-floor corridor, Harold and Eileen put out a range of not-very-inspiring potted plants. We attempted to restore the original stainless steel of the handrails on the stairs, connecting each of the three corridors, but with little success. Other blocks in the neighbourhood have banisters of highly polished brass, old Hollywood-style art deco. We couldn't match such glamour. Elena, The Orchard diva, had, during her reign at The Orchard, thrown a hissy fit at the bleakness of the entrance hall. 'How unwelcoming could a building be,' she had cried.

Nothing worked, even when Harold and Eileen

organised a communal painting event to brighten the gloom. Later Kim, our handyman, got hold of some old prints of urban London scenes. Designed to give character, though they hardly related to Orchard life. A job lot. Back of the lorry. They were probably part of a deal Kim did in the Black George on a Friday night. A return payment for services rendered. They are black-and-white photographs; the older ones sepia, all rather handsomely framed. Some go back to the turn of the last century, some as recent as the 1950s. Kim would have seen them as art pics and doubtless thought they could give the place a bit of class.

So here we are huddled together in the first-floor corridor. The ringleaders as usual are Bart and Emma from number eleven, the scene of the famous *Inspector Morse* episode. Joe from number eight downstairs rarely joins us for these Saturday-night affairs. After the daily morning hikes, his practice is to settle down to his painting. It's going well. The Hungarian family, later to become popular and gregarious, have been lying low during the first

Orchard Corridor pictures of London scenes, selected by Kim

year of lockdown. Jannis from number ten, painfully shy, is seldom spotted. That leaves (as well as Bart and Emma and their dog Darius) Emil, James and Simone and me.

As we assemble, we persuade ourselves that we are only slightly bending the rules. If indeed any of us can remember what the rules are, as we move into a second year of lockdown.

Most Saturday nights through January and February of 2021 and, my diary notes, even into March and April, we gather in the chilly space. We are denied the glorious spring, which kept us sort of sane last year. May is a washout. Later, through June and July, there is extreme weather from day to day, heat and cold, torrential rain. On the first Saturday, Emil produces an unspeakable cocktail. Emma does better the following week with an imaginative rendering of limoncello.

On the last Saturday of May, we abandon the Prosecco for champagne to celebrate Bart's return from Australia where he has managed a dramatic and complicated flight home to see his sick mum.

Each week we order in: fish and chips from Blue Ocean in Pitshanger Lane, tandoori or chicken tikka from Monty's, pizza from Santa Maria. Great in situ, inedible by the time it gets to The Orchard. Even the chicken tikka masala, famed as the best in West London, doesn't taste up to scratch after the motorcycle journey up Mount Park Road. Part of the corridor eating experience is that you never quite know what will turn up. On Pizza Night, I order what I think is a straightforward margherita – keeping it simple with mozzarella and basil – to get something strangely hot and peppery.

The Blue Ocean fish and chips wins by a mile.

Night falls

As night falls, we tell stories. If you type 'Ealing stories' into Google, you get 'Ealing Tories' or sometimes 'healing stories'. Most of us are not too interested in Ealing Tories, but we like the idea of 'healing'. Stories of kindness, humour, thoughtfulness. In this spirit, one Saturday in late February, I recount my experience of a few weeks earlier, on St Valentines Day. My diary entry reads: '14 February 2021. Freezing cold as I make my almost daily detour of our park. Snow has threatened all day and later it arrives, covering the two benches in The Orchard garden, the silver birch tree, the new shrubs planted by Laurie, an abandoned wheelbarrow. The two Hungarian boys hang out of the ground-floor window, showing off a freshly built snowman.

'On this St Valentine's morning, a mysterious elf has sprinkled messages on little cards all round the Arboretum. They are tucked into small bushes, attached loosely to trees, propped up on benches. They say: *You are loved. You are enough.*'

Not quite a haiku, perhaps a half haiku? I am not sure what 'enough' means here. But it has the right ring to it. 'Give yourself some slack'. 'You will do'. It's in the spirit of the much-loved poem by Mary Oliver, a favourite in our book group and which seems perfect for lockdown. Oliver's poem famously begins:

> *You do not have to be good.*
> *You do not have to walk on your knees*
> *for a hundred miles through the desert repenting.*
>
> From *Wild Geese* by Mary Oliver

One of the little cards in the park has been attached to a strawberry tree. After all the weeks of trying to record how many trees there are in the Arboretum, here was one I'd missed. Can strawberries really grow on trees? Whatever the case, I like this gift of love to passers-by. The gesture recalls Orlando in Shakespeare's *As You Like It*, who hangs poems to his beloved Rosalind on trees around the Forest of Arden. But these are better: love letters to everyone and anyone. *You are loved. You are enough.*

As the corridor darkens, we turn to less gentle stories, which tell of loss, horror, suicide, even murder. For the benefit of Orchard newcomers, Bart and Emma, the story of the crossbow murder – the one that took place in 1988 just round the corner in Stanley Court – is revisited and elaborated by Emil, with the addition of some blood-chilling detail. Not that this particular murder needed much embellishing. The incident was one of several local Agatha Christie-style murders. 'Crossbow' involved a jealous love rival, a murder committed in broad daylight, sightings of mysterious strangers.

The details are documented by well-known chroniclers of Ealing life, Paul Howard Lang and Dr Jonathan Oates:

> *Diana Stafford Maw was a thirty-six-year-old born in Northumberland and educated at the Cheltenham Ladies' College. She was found dead on the landing outside her flat in No 24 Stanley Court Ealing where she had lived since 1983. There was a crossbow bolt in her head.*
>
> Lang and Oates, 2020

That Diana was a posh girl, raised in the privileged setting of an exclusive girls' public school in the Cotswolds, and that the jealous love rival, though acquitted of the murder for lack of evidence, later set fire to her ex-boyfriend's home, adds an extra frisson to the tale.

There have been other unexplained Ealing deaths over the years which are, I decide, a touch too gruesome for a sociable Saturday night in the corridor. The body of an elderly gentleman, found years after his disappearance, in a rambling old house just down the road, by the cricket club. The swimming pool murder – like 'crossbow', another unsolved crime – also committed in broad daylight, in which the victim, Ruth Penelope Bell, was discovered in her blue Jaguar XJS in the car park of the local swimming pool.

> *The police investigation determined that Bell was a happily married and successful businesswoman, and could find no reason why anyone would want to kill her. Police believed that it was very likely that Mrs Bell knew her killer, but have struggled to ascertain a motive.*
>
> Wikipedia

For years I was reluctant to patronise the only public swimming pool in the area.

Often, we opt for more cheerful stories from around the world. Sometimes personal, sometimes political. So Simone talks about the influence of China in the country she originally comes from, Zambia. Emil, who has travelled widely in the Middle East, gives a hair-raising account of the danger of just trying to get from the airport to a hotel in downtown Tripoli. Emma tells the story of her Greek Cypriot parents immigrating to Australia, opening a fish and chip shop in Adelaide. Bart tells a different immigrant's tale – of his arrival in Australia, flying, as an abandoned baby, from Vietnam in a cardboard box. We already know the story from Bart's children's book *But What Are You?*, which describes Operation Babylift, a massive evacuation initiative in the 1970s, which saw over three thousand Vietnamese infants and children finding new homes across the globe through adoption.

More prosaic are my trips to Worthing and Uxbridge, both for funerals. The second is of a much-loved actor Arthur Cox. Arthur spent his last few years in Denville Hall, the famous nursing home for members of the theatrical profession near Uxbridge, and so the funeral is conducted by fellow actors – just short of camp and full of humour. The best we can manage by way of a wake is warm champagne in the crematorium car park.

And then there is teasing and joshing. A couple of weeks earlier, I had been sounding off – as I frequently do, it must be said. On this occasion, smugness is my theme, and the target – rather unfairly in recollection – is Richmond. We Ealingites tend to be rude about Richmond: well heeled, pleased with itself, all tennis coaches, yoga classes and wellness.

Simone and James tease me, after a now-rare trip to Richmond, recounting their exchanges during the visit.

'There's a smug person, James.'

'Yes, and that dog looks pretty smug.'

'And just see the group of people drinking on the lawn by the river – definitely smug.'

'Hang on, Simone, I've just spotted a *really* smug guy.'

'Wow, look at them, smugness written all over them… you cannot get smugger than that.'

And so it goes on.

Emil also weighs in. He has taken to lending me items from his extensive library. One is a book called *Cynical Theories*, an attack on critical theory. Emil knows that my university friends, especially my buddies in the Marx Reading Group, write things with titles like 'Queer Intersectionality'. Is he trying to wind me up, as a lefty academic? You never know with Emil.

At times, conviviality stalls, and I wonder again how we oddballs are thrown together in this circumstance. Even in normal times, we are not in and out of each other's homes. We are generally guarded, respectful of distance. Now even more so. I am seated on a chair in my doorway. It stands astride the threshold. Liminality taken literally.

Uncertainty. Not here or there. Neither in nor out – a metaphor of the way we are living our lives.

> *The Threshold seems like the place to be, not here or there, not one thing or another.*
>
> *The Promise* (Damon Galgut, 2021)

Only Darius, the Hungarian pointer, ignores the boundaries, wandering in and out of our neighbouring flats.

Corridors and courtyards

I have always liked the idea of shared spaces, not corridors so much as courtyards. In the communal space of my imagination, you assemble in the central arena, preferably with old and dear friends, but always with the option of retreat to private rooms, which encircle the courtyard.

Years ago, I stayed at a famous hotel in Jerusalem, planned around a shared courtyard. An academic friend

Shoshana Blum Kulka insisted there was no other place to stay in the city. When I checked out the history of the American Colony, it became clear why Shoshana, who died a few years ago and lived all her life in Jerusalem, had loved the place.

It seems that the building was originally built and owned by an Ottoman Pasha Rabbah Daoud Amin Effendi al-Husseini, who lived there with his harem of four wives. Soon after his fourth marriage, al-Husseini died, and the building was subsequently sold to a Christian group who arrived in Jerusalem in 1881 to set up a commune. Their leader was Horatio Spafford, a lawyer from Chicago, and his wife, Anna. The American Colony, as it came to be known, was later joined by Swedish Christians. The 'colony' engaged in philanthropic work amongst the people of Jerusalem, regardless of religious affiliation, gaining the trust of the local Muslim, Jewish and Christian communities.

Although the American Colony ceased to exist as a religious community in the late 1940s, individual members continued to be active in the daily life of Jerusalem, and in the 1950s, the society's communal residence was converted into the American Colony Hotel. The hotel became an integral part of the Jerusalem landscape where members of all communities in Jerusalem could meet. In 1992, representatives from the Palestine Liberation Organization and Israel met in the hotel, where they began talks that led to the historic 1993 Oslo Accord.

The American Colony has long since transitioned into just another luxury hotel, patronised by Hollywood stars, with photographs of Lauren Bacall and Bogart on its walls.

Interludes

Around this time, Ian in the book group sends me a poem which makes me look with fresh eyes at our corridor. Not arid emptiness, not unease or a sense of the unknown or hidden, but 'limbo' in the best sense of the word, a taking stock before we embark on the next life experience. Time to reflect, to embrace, not resist uncertainty. The final verse of the poem, which is called 'Interlude', reads:

> I too have rested here at these
> limbo interludes
> in our shared planet's rotation.
> So catch your breath and let my words
> welcome you like a friend's blessing.
> May this space around you expand
> and glow in the warmth of knowing
> that it's only a corridor;
> not a beginning, not an end,
> but a green oasis.

From *Interlude* by Debjani Chatterjee

BREXIT BLUES

We closed the borders folks, we nailed it
No trees, no plants, no immigrants
No foreign nurses, no doctors, we smashed it
We took control of our affairs. No fresh air.

From 'Planet Farage' by Jackie Kay

New Year's Eve 2020

A desultory firework display greets 2021. In The Orchard garden and organised by the stalwart Bart and Emma. The mood is bleak. The sadness is not just down to the Covid spike and the loss of Christmas but the final arrival of Brexit. Boris Johnson had promised something tough, not the wishy-washy affair on offer from Theresa May, the previous prime minister. But when it comes, on 31 January 2021, it isn't 'hard' after all – nothing so decisive and strong. Rather a wizened, feeble thing.

Hard, soft, soggy. Who cares? We are in mourning. Inspired by Jackie Kay's poem, I write my own lament, an imagined dialogue between a Remainer (me) and a Brexiteer.

ME: What of us, the so-called elite, who've 'had it so sweet'

all these years? While you dance in the street,
as you celebrate LEAVE, we grieve. It cannot be right
to celebrate loss.
BREXITEER: Loss of what? Of the Frogs and the
Krauts – who gives a toss?
ME: The British, who are they? Whatever the case,
they aren't us—
BREXITEER: Oh my what a fuss!
Stop remoaning, you and your sort –
come swallow your pride. Just be a good sport!

ME: Yes, we're not British – that much is clear –
BREXITEER: Oh no bloody fear – to be properly
British you're old and you're white.
ME: But I'm both!
BREXITEER: Well bad luck – hope you're up for the
fight –
long and bloody, the rest of your years.
You're buggered, you're skewered, my dears.
Meanwhile just welcome the sight of our heroes, Boris
and Nigel and Mogg,
as they dance in the street, with Dilyn the dog.

'Brexit Blues', Cathie Wallace

It's hard to find a Brexiteer at The Orchard. So many are from mainland Europe: Portugal, Hungary, Poland, Italy, Greece, Bulgaria. We are passionate Remainers. I know this because, though a Covid winter has brought isolation, we talked a lot during the temporary respite of the first lockdown summer, about Brexit and all sorts of things. I realise the sense of loss is to do with connectedness. Britain is about to cut itself loose and forgo the long-held goodwill from European friends. As Armando says, 'In Portugal, we used to admire the British: their pragmatism, common sense.' Armando is right. All that has gone. Now we have fatuous talk of an 'Australian' deal. This is feel-good stuff, as it evokes the Commonwealth, Queen and country and white countries. No one would boast about a 'Nigerian' deal or an 'Indonesian' deal. In the end we get a 'Canada-style' agreement. Few have a clue what this means.

And suddenly, Britain is a 'coastal state'. This is a term I never remember being used before. I deduce that it is all about fish. Forget financial services, let alone heavy industry, of which we have little left, it's true. Fisher folk, now central to our Britishness, and strongly Brexit, are the new local heroes.

It is still early January, and a squirrel is feasting on what could be the first shoots of our wild flower display. The seeds were planted by me and James back in September in the sort of garden below my bedroom window – that little patch encircled by Kim's famous wall.

A few days later and my diary entry of 13 January tells me that in the UK we have the highest ever daily death toll from Covid. On my little walk round the park, a young woman notices my gloom and my muttering about people pushing me into the very muddy grass. 'Jesus loves you,' she says. I'm sure she means well. But the last thing I need just now is a religious fanatic. And yes, it seems a bit harsh to equate my gentle fellow traveller in the park with the Trump madness. Still, I cannot but be reminded of the fact that, exactly a week earlier, on 6 January – after breaking in and smashing everything up – Trump supporters had formed a prayer circle in the Capitol building.

The jab

Still January and a new conversation, as we yell across the street or the park. 'Have you got your letter yet? Or was it a text? Where are you being done? Ealing Town Hall?' I shout over to Joe on his ever-more-ambitious daily hike, striding north today, towards Perivale, skirting the allotments off Pitshanger Lane.

'I'm the town hall, tomorrow.'

'Mine is Wembley Stadium, a drag to get to, but I'm not complaining.'

Indeed, no one complains. A spirit of gritty acceptance is abroad.

Today is the day of the jab. How does it feel? What does it signify? Who *doesn't* get it? We pretend it's not political, but of course it is. The Israelis have a brilliant vaccine roll-out. Only problem is that there is nothing for their Palestinian neighbours. Excited, I tell The Orchard folk – anyone who'll listen – that my turn has come. They smile and are pleased for me, particularly the charming newcomers in number nineteen, where Peter the Slovenian used to live, then Irene, the Russian, who was such fun but who vanished just before Covid arrived.

The first jab feels like a rite of passage. In spite of myself and the prevailing gloom, I feel a tiny bit more cheerful on my return from Wembley. Can you buck the system, jump the queue? Not really. There is still this British 'fair play' thing.

Then of course it's 'which one did you get?'

We are all stiff upper lip, saying with bravado, 'I'm quite happy with the Oxford one', as we called it then. This is even though the Swiss, Germans and Swedes are not giving it to their over sixty-five-year-olds and Macron has said it has something like a 15% success rate. That was until they decided that the French would *only* give it to the over fifty-five-year-olds and the Australians would not give it to anyone under fifty.

When I tell Emil that mine was the Oxford/AstraZeneca one, he says, 'Well, that one's not much more effective than a couple of Lemsips.'

Stoicism is the name of the game. My friend Elsa was offered either Moderna or Pfizer. Elsa, living in the United States, the country of choice – at least for the privileged – had options. But here in the UK we are proud to say, 'I'll take anything.' To be offered or to request choice doesn't seem quite the ticket. No one wants to rock this particular boat. Particularly as we agree that it is the one thing the country has got right. Bizarrely, Boris Johnson claims this success – as well as for himself of course – for capitalism. According to *The Sun*, Johnson has told his fellow conservatives, 'the reason we have the vaccine success is because of capitalism, because of greed, my friends'. For some of us, it is the contrary. No one likes to use the terms, but it is collectivism, dare I say *socialism*, at work. Even the Queen says, 'do it for others'.

Later, when more of us have had at least the first jab, we make bad, seaside-postcardy jokes.

'How was it for you?'

'Just a little prick,' says Emil.

'Great. And I had a cigarette afterwards,' says James, who has never smoked.

The jab leads to a very different conversation when Brzoska, my Polish cleaner and, I like to think, a friend, turns up in late January, after a few months of Covid-induced absence. Visibly shaken, she faces me. 'There's something you should know.' She looks at me: a steady, unflinching gaze. 'It's serious – very serious.' She hands me her smartphone. Thinking to be polite, I watch the video on her phone. It seems to feature an interview with someone who works for NASA. I make little sense of it, until the woman being interviewed says that implanted in human brains there are now robots designed to do the bidding of Bill Gates, who is promoting the vaccination programme for his own ends. On one level it strikes me as odd to point the finger at Gates. He's running the world anyway. He doesn't need to put chips in our arms or replace our brains with robots.

It seems that, at the core of anti-vaccine beliefs, is a conspiracy theory that vaccines do not work and/or are actively harmful, causing autoimmune disease, infertility in teenage girls, pretty much any of the world's ills. Indeed Brzoska, warming to her theme on this particular day, brings in the autism argument of Andrew Wakefield – the one that claims that the MMR jab, given to protect children against illnesses like mumps and measles, is linked to autism. Wakefield, completely discredited by the scientific community in the UK, hotfooted it to the US some years ago, where he was, until recently, feted as half of a celebrity couple with supermodel Elle Macpherson. It is no surprise that Wakefield is now claiming that the coronavirus is a hoax.

All of this raises issues as to what to believe. A few weeks after that first unsettling encounter, I lose my temper with Brzoska. 'I trust the medical profession,' I yell. But it's no good reasoning with her, as she thinks my brain has been replaced by a robot. I will not win this debate, because clearly it's not the original Cathie Wallace speaking but the implanted robotic brain, programmed by Bill Gates.

Later, I reflect that the question of who has the truth of the matter is more nuanced. It is painful for Brzoska to go against the views of her beloved sister, who texted the anti-vaxing video to her from Poland. Just as I cling to my old enlightenment mantra, embodied in a little quote by Georges Braque, which I come across around this time.

Truth exists, only falsehood has to be invented.

Georges Braque

Leaving aside the bigger epistemological questions of truth and falsehood, Patricia and I, who share the services of Brzoska, have practical things to resolve. There are ongoing intense discussions about how to 'handle' our vaccine-denying cleaner. My American friend Elsa, in her brisk, no-nonsense way, says 'she must go'. But we love Brzoska; I've known her for about twenty years. We've both lost track of just when she turned up on my doorstep, with the offer of work. She's family. She's also a good cleaner.

I opt for a good going-over with the Dettol after each visit, wiping every available surface. This is also irrational as there's no evidence of effectiveness there. At the same time, I escape for a trip round the park, during the couple of hours she cleans for me.

During one of my interludes in the park, I notice a new commemorative tree to a woman I knew only slightly but remember warmly. *Beryl Manly. Wife, mother and dedicated teacher*. I knew Beryl as an inspiring teacher at Montpelier School, which backs onto this little park.

Politics, pasta and a haiku for Chikayo

22 February and Luca is in philosophical mood today. The sun is out; we're chatting once again in the garden; and I'm ready for a bit of Italian. My efforts are clearly not up to much as Luca reverts quickly to English. As always with Luca, it's pasta and politics. I boast to him that I've recently extended my repertoire with Pesto Genovese – Luca is Genoese, and this is his local dish. Fortunately, he broadly approves my choice of ingredients. He can just about forgive my substitution of parmesan for pecorino. We move on to the terrible state of the world. He cannot get back to Italy just now of course, but the country is wrecked anyway, he says gloomily, ruined by Berlusconi. This was all before the even more disastrous intervention of the populist Italian politician Giorgia Meloni. Luca and I revisit the discourse about globalisation, the lack of hope for future generations and – a recurring theme – the disaster of Brexit. But the woes of the world pale in comparison to Luca's immediate problem of how his part-time job in the bagel shop in Earl's Court can support the rest of the family in number three.

Emil, meanwhile, is distraught. Chikayo in flat twenty, right above Emil's place, is going back to Japan. Chikayo was the perfect neighbour, working long hours at the Japanese School and, apart from that, just sleeping and eating. The two Latvian musicians who preceded her kept bohemian hours, never got home before two o'clock in the morning, always practising on the oboe and the cello.

We throw an impromptu party for Chikayo. We cheat as we are seven rather than the prescribed crowd of six and, aiming for some kind of distancing, huddle around the front porch, fortified with Prosecco and cheese. I do a haiku, not very inspired, but it triggers a new coinage: Orcharders. I had planned on Orchardians, but then I'd overshoot the permitted seventeen syllables. So I settle for the less elegant Orcharders.

A Haiku for Chikayo
Chikayo farewell,
We'll miss your charm and bright smile.
We Orcharders mourn.

Full circle
March, and in a few days, we will have come full circle, a whole year. A year in The Orchard. Not as glamorous as *A Year in Provence*, but we've come through it. Thousands round the country and beyond have documented their personal trajectory through the oddest year most of us have experienced.

In lockdown, complete strangers confide. 'I've been overthinking,' says the woman in front of me, as, masked and distanced, we queue to get into the surgery. This comment comes out of the blue, as if spoken to herself rather than the assembled company. Yes – overthinking, overeating and certainly overdrinking. My doctor's report confirms this, which brings on another haiku:

Blimey. I have to
Stop drinking. One G and T
A week. Says doctor.

So a miserable day. But there is a moment of joy when, out of my window, I see the blue tits making a nest in the heating duct below my sitting room window. This is a favourite spot, possibly because the heating is always on, as the radiator is behind an immovable sofa. I know spring is sort of coming when I see little heads peeking out, checking if the way is clear. That there is no chance of those pesky parakeets swooping in to snatch one of the chicks. Emma says that she can hear the tweeting from a similar duct right by her bedroom on the far side of the building.

A particularly handsome fox, not the cunning little vixen; this one with beautiful markings, a brownish brush with a very white tip to his tale. Sexist as we agree our assumption is, James and I are sure it is male. An enormous creature. A lion, says James. Only the upper part of his body is red; the rest is silver. He plays blissfully in the wasteland next door, before taking a snooze for the rest of a long afternoon.

David Attenborough has apparently said you need to just stand and listen for ten minutes in any piece of woodland. Just listen and look. I try this in Fox Woods but can only make out the parakeets and crows, whose racket drowns out everything else.

But suddenly success. Not in Fox Wood, but back in The Orchard garden. Birds I've never seen there before. Redwings – seemingly not rare but still I had to look them up. A black cap, goldfinches, scores of them, going mad, upside down in the silver birch outside my bedroom window. Then they're joined by a similarly deranged woodpecker, feasting on the catkins, dizzy with joy.

Bordello chic

It is May. We have staggered through winter and the loss of Christmas with a sort of spring emerging. The political shenanigans continue to play out in the wider world. Following poor results for Labour in the local elections, Johnson is still riding high in the opinion polls. There is the sense that the lives we inhabit are vastly different from those of our 'betters'. Much has happened in the year since that first May in 2020 when Dominic Cummings made the dash up north to his family home, followed by the notorious trip to Barnard Castle. He survived that debacle, only to leave the Johnson ménage in the autumn of the same year. My diary notes despair at the continuing popularity of the Tory prime minister, helped by the rollout of the vaccines. On 24 April, I had written: 'dispirited tonight. Do people really not care? Is it OK to be governed by a man without a shred of decency or integrity? Is that really OK?'

My mood is not helped by the sense that, as a nation, we are more divided than ever, north/south, metropolitan/rural, young/old. A national disaster, which some of us thought would bring us together in the old wartime spirit, has, rather than building solidarity, proved divisive. We Ealingites are part of the despised metropolitan bourgeoisie. OK, we don't inhabit the reviled North London, but West London is hardly better. Various kinds of coffee seem to get people going: decadent Londoners drink skinny lattes like Frasier Crane and his brother Niles in the nineties sitcom, *Frasier*.

It's hard to see how we are the privileged elite. Of course, many of us at The Orchard are fairly well heeled. But not all. Luca and his family certainly struggle. And there's plenty of poverty and hardship close to hand in a diverse borough like Ealing. Nonetheless, northern towns have undoubtedly fared worse, especially with Brexit promises fading. Hence the resentment towards the apparently more prosperous south. And I'm aware that there is an urban snootiness directed towards what have come to be called the 'red wall' towns, like Leigh in Greater Manchester, where I was brought up, now Tory supporting. I have done my share of sneering at these folk.

I decide to stop sneering.

But, even as I make this decision, lockdown boredom produces the temptation to have fun, to tease a little. When I bump into Emil or Joe around this time, popular targets are Boris and his fiancée Carrie and what came to be known, around May 2021, as 'Wallpapergate'. Towards the end of 2020, upmarket designer Lulu Lytle had been brought in to get rid of what was described as 'the John Lewis nightmare' left behind in the prime minister's quarters by Theresa May in 2019. Lulu, for a fee of £112,549.12, transformed the living quarters of 10 Downing Street. The gold wallpaper alone cost £850 a roll.

A few months later, Boris and Carrie marry, possibly to present a more respectable front at an upcoming international conference in Devon. Carrie Symonds is now Carrie Johnson (interesting that she has changed her name to his – no feminist there then). And what drives her to hitch her fortunes to a much older and not obviously attractive chap? We know little about her, other than her support for animal welfare. Also that she has expensive tastes. Well, perhaps taste is hardly the word. The glimpses we're allowed to see of the famed Lulu Lytle decor feature a lot of red plush, weird animal prints and Ottoman-style pouffes. A million miles away from the modest home decorating of most Orchard homes.

Bordello chic sums it up.

All of which makes one wonder about Mrs Johnson's own political ambitions. Not so much Margaret Thatcher, more Eva Perón, but badgers rather than the proletariat. Now she is Señora Johnson, I can see her waving from balconies. Johnson is not well groomed enough for General Perón. Clearly the hair is wrong, but Carrie J could clean up quite well as a Madonna version of Eva Perón in the musical *Evita*. I wonder if she can sing.

Although there were a few limp jokes about 'Carrie Antoinette' and 'let them eat wallpaper', the Wallpapergate story, leaking out at the height of Johnson's popularity, initially gained little traction. But later, at the end of 2021 and early 2022, it resurfaced as part of a growing narrative of Johnson's extravagance and irresponsibility. It was then that emails like the following emerged, the first addressed by Johnson to a Tory grandee who he is hoping to foot the not inconsiderable bill submitted by Lulu Lytle:

> *I'm afraid parts of our flat are still a bit of a tip and am keen to allow Lulu Lytle to get on with it. Can I possibly ask you to get in touch with her for approvals? Many thanks and all best Boris*

12.59pm, 29 November

The second is a spoof by John Crace of *The Guardian*, though so close to the Boris originals you'd hardly know:

> *Downing Street Flat is a complete tip. Just imagine the state that Theresa May left it in. The kitchen looks like something fitted by Peter Jones. I need an answer soonest Boris*

The Guardian, 7 January 2022

My kitchen at flat twelve *was* fitted by Peter Jones. I spent most of my retirement lump sum on it.

I would hardly expect to have much in common with the prime minister's young wife. What to her are the preferences of the despised lower middle class are to many of us – the petite bourgeoisie – the hallmark of good value and quiet good taste. For our generation, John Lewis (the parent store for Peter Jones) is a point of reference. In the sixties, my best friend Ruth Marks would boast of her Saturday job as a schoolgirl in the china department at the Oxford Street store, as much a source of pride as her university place to read English at King's College, London. Her mum was in lingerie for years, finally getting sacked at the age of eighty, because – keen to keep the job she loved – she'd lied about her age.

It follows that on 7 May 2021, my first tube trip and retail experience for well over a year is to a John Lewis store. The closest to me is the Peter Jones in Sloane Square. Also the District line is a bit airier, with walk-through carriages, no risky changes, no lifts. I'd planned for an orgy of spending but can only manage several sets of socks, the underwear I always choose and a replacement pair of joggers. I do a quick scout round the store and take the District line back to Ealing.

The loose trousers and baggy knickers are now essential items. *The Guardian* proclaims how lockdown has 'changed body image'. It has certainly changed body shape, as witnessed by rolls of comforting fat nestling around our waistlines. I appear to have a part of my anatomy which simply was not there before, an interesting flap of flesh around my lower abdomen. The John Lewis joggers are the only option. I'm not alone. Well, that is apart from Joe, sleek and trim, with his new regime, which takes him on his route marches across the borough. And James, lean as a whippet from the workouts organised by Bart, who of course is himself in terrific shape, proud of the physique that served him so well as an extra in the successful BBC series *Bodyguard.* At times I almost trip over James sprawled in The Orchard corridor, performing Bart's regime of daily press-ups.

WHAT IS TO BE DONE?

We are marching… along a precipitous and difficult path,
firmly holding each other by the hand.

What Is to Be Done? (Vladimir Lenin,1902)

19 July 2021

Freedom day, on 19 July, has been much heralded by
Boris Johnson. For many of us, it is seen as, at best,
another publicity stunt; at worst, a day of fear rather than
freedom for elderly and vulnerable people or those with
compromised immune systems. Certainly the occasion
is underwhelming in the Lane. A disconsolate feel. Few
people around. Pitshanger Village Bakery closed due to
Covid infection, for the only time since the beginning of
the first wave.

Two days earlier, on 17 July, I had received the email
one dreads. Our book group researcher Henry (Henry
was studying the therapeutic effects of community
reading groups) emails to say that he has tested positive
for Covid and has symptoms. The plan had been,
anticipating 'freedom day', that this would be the first
day back for 'normal' face-to-face life, when we resumed
our book group meetings at Ladbroke Grove Library.

Woefully underfunded, the library has long experienced a series of problems. On this occasion there had been a flood in the basement, so it was closed. Our little group, including Henry, Denise and Kamla, seen previously only on Zoom, huddled outside over coffee at the dingy cafe next door.

On the 19th, I pick up my self-testing kit from the pharmacy, a routine which is later to become almost a way of life. On the way home I'm comforted by the wonderful smell of the lime tree blossom in the park. There is a narrow window of opportunity in which to experience this, a matter of days during which the scent is overwhelming, before it swiftly subsides. It seems I haven't missed it this July, as feared. My arboreal knowledge is so limited that I hadn't been sure whether those little sprouts were flower buds or seeds. Things coming or going.

It is Saturday and barbecue night. The party activity starts early in the garden, but I decide to give it a miss. I feel strung out and uneasy about any kind of socialising.

I do the test, it is negative and I trot down to the garden, announcing from the safety of Kim's famous wall (the one he dedicated to Donald Trump – ironically, I should add) that I won't get closer. It is a perfect evening: there is an easy tolerance, no ranting, no political stuff (often from me, it must be said). We move comfortably from one conversational cluster to another. I love the diversity of age – from seventy-eight to three – of ethnicity, languages and social class. I love that Balint, Amin and Gergő let little Clara play football with them, though she keeps running off with the ball. This bothers the boys not a jot.

I'm cautious. Should I be here at all? I still haven't got

the official notification to isolate but even so... I feel guilty. Half there and half not. But Joe says, as I eye the sausages on the grill, 'Go for it, Cath.'

August and more gossip

It is August, the one hot week of the year. I'm out of isolation and reading my homework in the garden, in preparation for our Zoom meeting of the Marx Reading Group. Suddenly, Andrzej creeps up on me. Months pass when Andrzej is barely visible, and then suddenly he is ubiquitous. Always apparently ecstatic to see me and inexhaustibly curious, he pounces.

Andrzej: 'Cathie, how lovely. What are you reading?'

Cathie: 'Er... *What Is to Be Done?* Lenin.'

A: 'Of course. I know it.'

That Andrzej doesn't miss a beat is not surprising. Not just because of his genuinely prodigious knowledge, but because he would have been schooled in Communist-era Poland and almost certainly is more conversant with socialist literature than I am. The next day, trying to negotiate the hosepipe to fulfil the promise of watering the roses, during what is now a heatwave, I again bump into Andrzej out the back, this time with his grandson Jake. On the third occasion, he is firing up one of his fleet of vintage cars, what I call the Grace Kelly one – identical to that which, according to Emil, featured in her iconic film *High Society*. The fumes are overwhelming. As I chide him, I exploit my moral advantage to ask if I can interview him about my Orchard project. Ever good-humoured, Andrzej complies.

The brief summer has brought respite from the corridor; the rules finally allow some cautious indoor socialising. So we agree to meet one evening in his lovely house round the corner from The Orchard.

Andrzej is characteristically generous, both with the offer of good wine and his willingness to talk for hours. Which we do. He has a gift for hyperbole, adding colour and detail to many of the stories I already know in outline, mainly about the Old-Timers, all now dead. As Andrzej warms to his theme of 'the old days', Hulda, Jan and Gerald are elevated in status and nobility. Certainly, Hulda had held a senior job with the local council in children's services. I knew that – but now, in Andrzej's narrative, she single-handedly supported orphan children and played a major part in the war effort, where she had learnt how to be a nifty mechanic. Gerald, says Andrzej, had spotted her mending a car in one of the garages out the back. I wasn't aware that she could drive.

I had known that Jan was a war hero, married to a former beauty queen who cared for him, even after their divorce. I too had witnessed 'Maria's devotion to the end, sitting there day and night' in the nursing home where Jan spent his final days. But I didn't know that he was a skilled horseman, one of the last cavalrymen to serve in the Polish Army. It seems that the Polish cavalry continued to use the lance for training purposes up to the outbreak of the Second World War. Hence the presence of a lance, as witnessed by Andrzej, in Jan's Orchard flat.

'Before the war, he was in the cavalry school. This was the period when the cavalry became mechanised, so they went from the horse to the tank. He was interned during the war, and then after the war, the armed division ended up in Germany. And he was there for a long time, competing in equestrian competitions. Whilst in London, he met this girl, Miss Polonia, a most beautiful girl.

'He still had a lance; he had all the cavalry books from before the war. He didn't move on. His world stopped in 1945.'

Andrzej turns to tales of his much-admired friend Gerald Horrocks. Gerald's funeral eulogy had told us that this 'adventurer, soldier, schoolmaster, traveller' had served as a captain with the British Army in East Africa. But I didn't know that, at one point, Gerald, as an accomplished athlete, was called upon to take an urgent message across Africa.

Andrzej continues the story: 'Gerald Horrocks – before the war – was running marathons. As a courier he was sent to Lake Victoria. He was a long-distance runner. He was just amazing. I know also that, when he was running to Lake Victoria, it was because they ran out of postal pigeons.'

How can you run out of pigeons?

If the heroes become more heroic in Andrzej's stories, the down-and-outs are downer and outer. Diana, the sad lady with the dog in flat fifteen, even though promoted from a writer of short stories to Poet Laureate in Andrzej's account, is remembered as a hopeless alcoholic, brewing *poitín* (home-made liquor) in the top-floor corridor.

'She was alcoholic, brewing *poitín* on the landing on the top floor. *Poitín* is Irish for home-made alcohol. When we arrived, Gerald Horrocks told me, "We've got this special situation: we've got a Poet Laureate" – Gerald was convinced she was Poet Laureate – "but she's also an alcoholic."'

Kim's life story is similarly embellished as the night wears on. I had thought he was a working-class local boy. But Andrzej insists he went to the prep school just a few blocks from The Orchard, the one where Gerald Horrocks was Assistant Headmaster. I demur. That cannot be right. Wrong accent. 'An Englishman is branded on the tongue,' as John le Carré once said. But Andrzej insists. The family had money and Mum was posh.

'Kim was very much under the influence of his mother, who was incredibly elegant. She used to come to The Orchard. Mum was very smartly dressed, and she sounded very well educated – she had a privileged education.'

Certainly, Kim wished to present himself as more than a handyman when he first arrived at The Orchard, as Andrzej indicates: 'He advertised in the BBC magazine as a "bespoke carpenter".'

He was also an avid reader. 'He had tons and tons of books, usually paperbacks that other people had thrown away.'

Andrzej goes on to chart Kim's decline. 'Many years after, he became very sloppy. I recommended him to my daughter because he needed work. He went to her house, and it was an absolutely botched job, and so she would never use him again afterwards. But, having said that, if you needed someone on 31 December or on Christmas day, he would be there.

'He used to come and sit here [in Andrzej and Ewa's house], drink his cup of tea, talk to Ewa and talk to me. He was a lonely man. He was an alcoholic, but he knew the difference between a good bottle of wine and a bad bottle of wine. He used to give me instructions on what he wanted when I offered a Christmas gift.

'The kitchen [in his White City flat] was full of washing lines. And there were masses of badly washed stuff that was drying. I cannot swear there were not cockroaches there. He lived in very unhygienic and pretty bad conditions… he didn't have a pension. His day would finish at one o'clock. He would go to the pub. He was a regular at the pub at the very beginning of Ducane Road. Everyone knew him over there. He was also a handyman in this pub, broken toilets – that kind of thing. He liked to win arguments – if he was on the sober side. It would be slightly different if he was drunk. He was banned, and so he moved fifteen metres to the next pub up the road, and he eventually ended up being banned from all the pubs, apart from Black George.'

Andrzej and I agree that we miss him.

Andrzej: 'You don't find another Kim easily.'

Cathie: 'He could work out the problem. He knew what needed to be done.'

A: 'Even when he was sitting there in his cubby hole [the shed in The Orchard garden]. Always rolling his cigarettes.'

C: 'He's missed.'

Goulash, picnics and farewells

Late summer, September. Over what is coming up for eighteen months, a whole new life has sprung up in our Arboretum, the little park next to The Orchard. People used to cross the park swiftly and purposefully. The young and healthy can do it in two strides. It takes me exactly five minutes to encircle it at a modest pace. I've timed it. In the early lockdown days, with the mantra of 'at least twenty minutes of brisk daily exercise' in mind, I aimed for four laps. Later, people lingered. We became less driven, more relaxed. Today a young woman is boxing, sparring with her trainer on the grass. A few days ago, an equally elegant couple were fencing. This is all new to this public outdoor arena.

Pilates groups, Keep Fit, yoga meetings, earlier out of sight, are all now on display. And, as I see kids rushing around in smart uniforms, I wonder if they are Cubs. Do we still have those? The children seem very small, and a bit of research uncovers a new group, 'Squirrels', a programme for four- to six-year-old children. The adults have brought in their own folding chairs, aiming for more settled residence. Lovers find a spot. And then, for a few weeks in July, there had been the mighty splendour of the lime, so heavily burdened with its blossom, the ranger had said, that it might one day collapse under its own weight.

At The Orchard, the exchange of goods and services continues. Joe decorates Simone and James's flat while they are away in Ireland, the first trip since lockdown. Each afternoon, I toss my *Guardian* on their doormat, occasionally bringing croissants from the Pitshanger bakers. The croissants go down better than *The Guardian*, which is a bit too lefty and self-congratulatory for James.

Luca, Riccardo and Valentina are leaving for a bigger, but probably cheaper, rented house in Southall, just opposite the hospital, thus handy, jokes Valentina, as the family are frequent visitors to Accident and Emergency. I caught Luca one day waiting for an ambulance to take him to Ealing Hospital. His blood pressure was a little raised, he explained. As a fellow hypochondriac, I sympathised, aware too – at the risk of stereotyping – of a national tendency among Italians. I always remember Ausonio Zappa, my boss when I worked in Rome, appearing in a sling. Asked why, he explained he had suffered a *colpo d'aria*, roughly translated as 'sitting in a draft'.

A cup of tea in the garden, planned to mark the departure of the Italians, has progressed into full-scale goulash. Eszter appears at my back door in great excitement. Have I got a saucepan big enough for twelve people?

Goulash. Is this taking multiculturalism too far? For the new-in-lockdown TV news outlet GB News, 'multiculturalism' is one of the despised *m*'s, as I call them: the hardcore GB presenters hate – in no particular order – Meghan Markle, masks, Marxism, millennials and multiculturalism. And Marcus. They detest the young footballer Marcus Rashford, for 'taking the knee' at the start of matches. But in view of his enormous popularity, they have to play that down a bit. I devise tongue twisters to amuse myself, along the lines of: masked Marxist millennial, Meghan Markle, marched with Marcus in support of multiculturalism.

Lorenzo – 'the kid' as Luca calls him – has broken his arm. He is a sweet but pampered boy who doesn't get involved in the rough-and-tumble football with Gergő and Balint, Arin and little Clara. Riccardo puts a fatherly arm round him as he, Luca and Valentina crowd onto Kim's seat.

Eszter's mum Eva is visiting from Hungary. Even though she has to quarantine pretty well the whole period of the trip, she is able to supervise the goulash and join us from a distance in the garden. She gives me a tiny packet of paprika as a parting gift, before she leaves the next morning. I recall that my one attempt at cooking goulash

(Eileen's recipe) was disastrous, so I sense some culinary opportunity here.

Unusually, Joe is there this evening. We had talked a few nights earlier in the garden, not politics this time but painting. Joe talks passionately and compellingly about the painters he most admires:

'Rembrandt. Goya knocks me out. Picasso. Sometimes I think I don't really like him, and yet other times he blows me away. Freud's good and all. A lot of people put him down. But you can just love his paint. On some of his necks... it's just to die for. The paint... what I get out of a painting. It's almost like Bacon. I like Bacon beyond his image – I like his placement of colour and his balance and the abstract nature of his painting. I think he's the most genius painter that has ever been on this earth. You stand in front of one of his paintings and, er, the balance and the colour – it's just perfect.'

Some time later, there is an exhibition of Lucian Freud's work at the Royal Academy in Piccadilly. Five-star reviews. I am reminded of Joe's words, as I stand in front of the wonderfully fleshy nudes. I pay particular attention to necks.

Rear window

Late summer and a new lockdown wave looms. More time to sit and stare. My bit of The Orchard offers access to many windows, not just those of our block but further afield. More than ever do I serve the role of curtain twitcher, voyeur. I am reminded of Hitchcock's *Rear Window*, as shadowy figures flit back and forth at dusk, before curtains or blinds close.

We neighbours are near strangers and yet intimate.

In closer than usual contact, we know about daily routines, when people get up, go to bed, time spent in the bathroom, as lights go on and off. Gergő and Balint's bedroom, directly below my study, tells me they are still up late – they are allowed an hour's reading before lights off. Hanna's elegant arm reaches through her downstairs window on the ground floor each morning when she feeds the squirrels.

I think of Hanna one day when a squirrel comes right up to the sill of my first-floor flat. This has never happened before, and I'm sure the animal thinks that food is on offer.

One house out the back is different from the more typical suburban homes. A local architect built it for his family and, far from being the feared eyesore, it is full of light and laughter; children playing; parties that are joyous, never rowdy. A house of glass and timber. No coverings on the enormous windows. It is open to view. Generous.

And now there is a new house arising from the former wasteland next door. Nimby-wise, we tried to stop it. Emil was particularly exercised in this endeavour. But to no avail.

My days, over late summer and autumn of this second year of lockdown, are spent watching the construction evolve. Post-Brexit and post-Covid, there is a shortage of skilled labour. Many of the Eastern Europeans have headed home. This might explain why Barnaby and his team of brickies come every day from Portsmouth on the South Coast. So Barnaby tells me, when he drops by at number twelve to introduce himself.

One morning, I hear a woman's voice. I peer through my bedroom window. Girl or woman, I'm not sure. I recognise her by the jaunty topknot that ties up her hair.

Pretty face and neat features, but weather worn. She is carrying a massive pile of bricks up a ladder. The guy takes them from her, as she reaches the top. *OK, but why doesn't he do the ladder bit*? I wonder. That must be harder. The girl is graceful but tough. Strong thighs, I note. Footballer's legs perhaps, as it seems that Barnaby met her playing in the local Hampshire team.

James calls it the Pyramid. This is testament to the building's impressive scale and the many hours of sweated labour spent on its construction. But it is more of a castle, with turrets and interesting architectural flourishes. Recently, porthole windows have been added, which brings to mind an ocean-going liner. Perhaps one day it will sail away to foreign shores. I will wake up to the former tranquillity of the lovely wild garden.

Meanwhile, nature is out of joint. Birds are confused. A lone thrush has clearly lost its way (we never see thrushes in The Orchard garden) as it attempts to land on the unyielding surface of the Pyramid. A woodpecker seems to think it is a strange new kind of tree, as it pecks fruitlessly at the unforgiving wall. Only the magpies pose majestic, in charge, on the battlements.

Part Three

AND SO IT ALL WENT ON

And so it all went on… we did not leave.

The Memoirs of a Survivor, (Doris Lessing, 1974)

2022

It is over forty years since I first had sight of The Orchard. Then a settled community of what I came to call the Old-Timers; later, with the arrival of the New Cosmopolitans, a multicultural microcosm – people of all kinds flung together by chance.

The building itself is remarkably unchanged since 1981. The funny canopy over the front door remains. It has been tarted up from time to time, but there is still the look of a slightly dodgy hotel. Yes, there is the addition of the carpet in the corridors, making the place bleaker rather than cosy; on the walls the prints of London scenes, which Kim installed not long before he died. Signs of children in the foyer, absent in the early days, with pushchairs, a battered-looking hobby horse and, along the corridors, tiny shoes next to adult ones on doormats, the spillover from small flats.

Number twelve has also remained much as it was when I moved in. I hang on to the original steel-framed

Shoes outside a door

windows and the old bathroom tiles in the belief that they 'retain the style of the flat'. I continue to skewer my elbows on the sharp-cornered door handles. I shudder at the horror of the old gas fire, long out of operation, but cannot contemplate its removal.

I eventually made a few concessions to change when my old cast-iron bath was dismantled (it took three strong men to get it down the stairs). At about the same time, Ian's keyboard piano moved into the already cluttered spare room. After a twenty-six-year unblemished tenancy, Ian, my Bookbreak buddy, had been evicted from his flat, with nowhere to put a lifetime of treasured possessions. He himself had to move from Kilburn to a grotty room in Holloway.

But that all came later. In 2022, we Orchardians were still dealing with the fallout from Covid. At first a matter of weeks, then 'three months', we were told. The elderly were to be particularly affected, as much more vulnerable to the new virus. Leading at the time to jokes about 'locking up the oldies'. My friends and I joined in the merriment, the absurdity. Surely not? Stoically, we knuckled down. Until we thought, perhaps a year? Then – maybe till summer? And so it went on.

It is now 17 March 2022 – two years to the day since I started my diary with the words: 'a virus, a simple virus, an accident of nature, has the power to destroy lives and wreck world economies. Already the streets of the major world capitals are empty'.

New times

There has been a heightened sense of time passing, but also standing still. A seamlessness. What we had thought of as finite is now open-ended.

> When the coronavirus pandemic started most of us naively assumed that it would have an end. We would know when it was over.
>
> Gaby Hinsliff, *The Guardian*, 26 February 2022

For many, the suspension of time is tricky. We are inclined to feel we have to 'do things' with our lives. Have purpose, goals, meaning. Covid has taken away personal agency and control over day-to-day planning. Are we faced with opportunity or loss? A time to write the bad novel or emptiness and aimlessness? 'The lost two years of our lives', writes one friend in her Christmas letter.

New spaces

Space too has taken on new meaning. The Orchard corridor on the first floor: once a convenience, a conduit, a route from one place to another, is now a space in its own right. It has become the place not just of Saturday-night get-togethers, but of tea parties to celebrate birthdays, such as Simone's recent fortieth, and Bart's daily exercise classes. Following the success of the Serbian spruces at

Orchard bookcase

Christmas – well, two Christmases now – which occupied a corner of the ground-floor foyer, we now have a corridor bookcase, making use of that bit of dead space just outside my flat. Everyone, particularly the children (Gergő is a keen reader), can help themselves to any book they like, says James, whose idea this is.

Schools are also using space differently, pushing the kids to more outdoor learning and out of crowded classrooms. There is a recently appointed 'outdoor specialist' at Grantham Primary School in Ealing, along with a new 'reading chalet' in the bit of wasteland out the back, which was formerly used for not very much. There are few volumes so far (they have to be hardback because paperbacks quickly get mouldy), but the timber smells beautiful. It is like settling down with a book in an alpine forest.

Pretty much every evening, around seven o'clock, I hear pounding and groaning just outside my front door.

I recognise Bart's voice, but Emma, Simone and James are there too.

'Good.'

'Give it to me.'

'Beautiful.'

'Three, two, one, *go!*'

'Hang on, hang on.' Emma giggles.

'Use your legs. Use your legs!'

'Forty seconds left. Come on. Come on.'

Little Clara from flat twenty, attracted by the music, gets in the way of the boxers and lifters. Simone extends a long, graceful arm to keep her safe from the heavy weights. It occurs to me, not for the first time, that, while we are constrained, children and Darius run around freely.

As so often, I have, as the incompetent anthropologist, got things wrong. My sexist assumption was that it was the men doing the corridor weightlifting and boxing. All wrong. Emma is a mean boxer, Simone too.

I spy all this through the keyhole in my front door.

It's not just the corridor that has been reclaimed as a new space, but the garden. BL – Before Lockdown – the garden was used only for the occasional barbecue, sunbathing by the Wild Girls and a bit of haphazard gardening, if someone got the urge. During the first glorious lockdown spring, it was recommissioned for all kinds of other activities: Hanna's yoga, more vigorous workouts than are feasible in the corridor, of the kind that might involve swinging on the poor little oak tree. And of course, the rehearsed reading of Bart's children's book *But What Are You?*

And then there were the New Year's Eve parties when being indoors together still felt unsafe. At least 2022 is a jollier affair than the previous year's muted celebration. Bart runs around festooned in fairy lights, a mobile Christmas tree. An overexuberant Catherine wheel whizzes out of control, leading us to hope it might set fire to the Pyramid, otherwise known as The House Next Door, the unwelcome post-lockdown replacement of the former wilderness.

Masks, mayhem and metaphors

Part of the ambivalence we are living with, the 'will we, won't we?', 'should we, shouldn't we?' is the matter of masks, now heavy with symbolism. No longer just bits of cloth you wear over your mouth and nose.

We Orchard folk tend not to use cars. We walk or cycle. James frequently heads off on his butch motorbike. And we take buses and the tube. Here the mask madness kicks in. For Londoners the issue arises, as we begin to venture out again into the world, of which feels safest: black cabs, minicabs, Ubers, trains – overground or underground – or buses. And the climate of uncertainty is not helped by the fact that, while the central government has withdrawn any regulations, Transport for London is still advising, in March 2022, the use of masks. Mixed messages all over the place. And mixed reactions. As Emma says, 'In London [during the early lockdown days], there were beautiful acts of kindness and attempts to galvanise things when people were feeling so down. Not just here but around the world. But then I think they became fatigued, Covid fatigued, mask fatigued. People started to push the guidelines a bit, started to become sceptical, started to become cynical.'

We had hoped for a coming together, solidarity, that what Emma called the 'beautiful acts of kindness' would endure. But my hope for the revival of the public sphere, of a sense of the collective – 'we're all in this together' kind of thing – now seems something of a lost hope.

The triumph of individualism is typified by the mask business. It's such a small matter, one would think, to wear a mask for a twenty-minute journey, in order to make fellow passengers feel a bit more comfortable, even if you feel they are deluded. But no, for the mask-averse, it's a God-given right *not* to wear a mask, a weird kind of reversal of the similar mantra of the gun-carrying Americans, whose freedom is posited on the right *to* – most significantly to carry a weapon. 'I don't feel it is necessary' to wear a mask, proudly proclaims my favourite Channel GB anchor Michelle Dewberry. An odd example of the 'virtue signalling' the mask haters despise so much.

Back in 2021, in the early days of the mask debate and taking the first tentative steps back into my old travelling life, I had conducted a little experiment. Coming back to Ealing from town, three mask-less people in turn had sat down opposite me. The first, a young woman, was hostile. 'I'm exempt,' she said, with an empty, challenging stare. She was replaced at South Kensington by a young man, similarly mask-less. When challenged, this chap grudgingly put on an enormous, rather splendid mask. The third, another young man, looked blank. 'I don't have one,' he said, as though he had never heard of such a thing, before shuffling off down the carriage.

A few weeks later and another mask story. I asked politely (I'm always polite): 'Would you mind possibly…?'

The young woman replied in a perfectly pleasant way, 'So sorry, I don't have one.' At this point, the woman sitting opposite us offered her a disposable one. She had a whole stack of them in her handbag. Young woman accepted it. Job done.

For some, a mask says 'compliant', 'totalitarian'. 'Do you want to be like Communist China?' A certain kind of Tory gets particularly hot under the collar about mask wearing. 'Nothing would make me less likely to go shopping than the thought of having to mask up,' Tory MP Desmond Swayne rallied in the House of Commons today. The MP for New Forest West argued that this is a 'monstrous imposition against myself and a number of outraged and reluctant constituents'. (It's not clear whether Swayne's outrage applies to all face coverings: the MP has happily admitted to wearing blackface at a fancy-dress party in the past.) Steerpike, *The Spectator*, 14 July 2020.

Jacob Rees-Mogg is another well-known anti-masker. The Tory grandee is a bit of an easy target for us lefties, as he frequently snoozes on the government front benches. Later, when Mogg finally yields (for about a week he is sighted wearing a mask in the House of Commons), I cannot resist another ode.

Have you seen it? Tell everyone. Mogg's in a mask
–
A manly, black, handsome one, if you're tempted to ask.
Our Jacob, adored by the right, nay, seen as a light
In the darkness of wokery – all that
Jiggery pokery.
Now sits the great man on his pew in the House.
A man of few words, oft quiet as a mouse.
But, lo, today wearing – I'm swearing –
A MASK.

What the f...?! you might ask.
Libertarian – in the land of the free –
Where it's never the us, just the me, me and me.

Cathie Wallace

Burns Night – the fight back

As a way of countering the individualism of the mask refuseniks and celebrating the collective Orchard spirit, Burns Night, which is always on 25 January, seemed a good idea. The Burns Night tradition at number twelve had started some years earlier, around the same time as my colleagues and I at UCL launched the Marx Reading Group. After all, Robert Burns was a socialist, whose poems, songs and letters reveal a revolutionary, on the side of the poor and oppressed. Of course, everyone has, for some time now, appropriated Burns. Lots of posh Scots (well, often not even Scots) in kilts all over London. Not a socialist thought in their heads.

So, as January 2022 beckoned, I had thought that there was no harm in claiming Burns back for hard times. Out of the question in the heavier lockdown of 2021, but we might just risk a corridor version this year.

With Burns Night comes haggis, which requires some kind of introduction to many of the newer Orchardians. Bart has heard of it, may even have tasted it, but is squeamish. Eszter says that there is something very similar in Hungary. I wonder, recalling the wild party of the Soviet students all those years ago, if it is of the *plov* family. Gergő insists on knowing exactly how it is made. Checking my facts on Wikipedia, I tell him: 'Haggis is a savoury pudding containing sheep's pluck, minced with onion, oatmeal, suet, spices and salt, mixed with stock and cooked while traditionally encased in the animal's stomach.'

There is further clarification needed around the haggis accompaniments. There has to be mashed potato and swede, not a familiar vegetable, but essential to add a bit of yellowness to the general look of grey sludge.

A problem arises. We need a Scot to read Burns' 'Address to a Haggis'. I qualify, but only after a fashion: my father's side are all Irish/Scottish, but I cannot do lowland Scots with any kind of conviction. James's Ulster lilt comes closest. So he is lined up for the role of Reader of the Address and equipped with the knife to pierce the skin of the haggis, at the moment it appears gloriously displayed on its platter. He spends some time rehearsing.

'The groaning trencher there ye fill,

'Your hurdies like a distant hill.'

Hurdies means 'buttocks' in modern standard English, which seems exactly right to describe the two large foil-wrapped haunches, nestling side by side in my oven. They've been cooking (heating up, really, as they are already cooked) for hours.

I nervously pat the large pillows of minced meat coming out of the oven. Well, not exactly meat: offal, oatmeal and suet, snug in the mandatory sheep skin. They are suspiciously soft and spongy as I peel away the foil. Emil and I manoeuvre the first monster onto a plate, but the beast slips between us to land on the kitchen floor. I'm distracted by little Clara who has escaped into my living room. Doubtful that the floor would pass the 'five-second rule', we nonetheless scoop up what we can and attempt some kind of arrangement on the platter.

James – never one to be put out by minor hitches – gives a full-throttle Donald Wolfit performance. He stands grandly on the flight of stairs going down to the entrance hall. A rarely seen Thespian James. In a sonorous roar he proclaims:

'His knife see rustic Labour dight,

'An cut you up wi ready slight,

'Trenching your gushing entrails bright,

'Like onie ditch;

'And then, O what a glorious sight,

'Warm-reekin, rich!'

In the event, there is not much of a 'glorious sight' and no 'gushing entrails'. Though James embarks manfully on the 'Address to a Haggis' and the knife is poised to pierce the smooth, gleaming creature, it is all for nothing. The skin has already burst. The unappetising bladder of the dead haggis droops sadly on the dish.

But if culinarily – is that a word? – a disaster, multiculinarily, the night can be claimed a triumph, as all sorts of other food show up, suggesting there has been some initial apprehension about the haggis. An odd mixture of jelly, spare ribs, unusual crudités, as well as the pavlova that Eszter always does. Obvious Russian influence there. The chocolate mousse is a Portuguese version: more eggs to make it lighter, fluffier, says Anna. Multiculturally, the night is also a success. Eighteen adults and five children of twelve different ethnicities, nationalities and languages, including Bulgarian, Polish, Portuguese, Hungarian, Shona and Temba. This triggers the thought that the new corridor library has to have books not just in English but in all the languages represented in our block of flats.

That night, unable to sleep because of the haggis debacle, I count the number of neighbours who have shown up. Everyone was invited. Like counting sheep, I count my neighbours. After nearly two years in lockdown, who in our eighteen flats at The Orchard has left and who remains?

Flat three: still empty since the Italian family departed. Luca keeps in touch by email, so I know the family have settled well into the new house in Southall and Lorenzo likes his new school. Valentina is planning to do a course at the local university.

Flat four: a new couple there – the Amazon packages suggest, from the names, that they are of Chinese heritage.

Flat five: Anna and Armando – resident for so many years that, though still young, they almost count as Old-Timers.

Flat six: Tamás, Eszter, Balint and Gergő.

Flat seven: Hanna and her boyfriend Ziggy.

Flat eight: Joe.

Our six flats on the first floor haven't changed apart from rather mysterious new tenants in flat nine. There is still – going clockwise from flat nine at the front – quiet Jannis, Bart and Emma of course, me, James and Simone and Emil.

At this point I fall asleep but later recall changes on the top floor. The young doctor Kutzei and her partner Zac, whom I'd bumped into one evening a few weeks earlier, have moved into flat fifteen. Ivan and Maggie, with daughters Clara and Octavia, are in flat twenty. Ivan is in IT and Maggie is Chief Buyer for H&M down the Broadway. And two Aussies, Ben with his British partner Olivia from flat sixteen and glamorous Kristina Kellaway in flat nineteen, who turns out to be a rather good soul singer, though her day job is as a visiting academic, teaching music at the University of West London.

It had been good to talk to some of the newer folk at the Burns Night, previously spotted only in passing. Teacher Ben, married in lockdown to Olivia, hasn't heard of Robert Burns, though he knows William Wallace, made famous of course in the film *Braveheart*. Fuelled by the Irish whisky we prefer to Scotch, Ben discloses some of the coded ways teachers have of hinting to the ambitious parents at the private school where he teaches (the usual footballers and pop stars) that their kids are not quite as seriously gifted as they'd hoped. Kutzei, whose family come from Zimbabwe, talks about the punishing periods of duty she has to do at Hillingdon Hospital. She's only joined us as, arriving late from her shift, she bumped into the merriment on the stairs. Local elections are approaching in May and Ivan who, as a council tax payer, can vote – though not in national elections – assumes that local councillors are in it for the money, surely? 'Well, yes and no,' I say. 'They do get handsome expenses, but they do not receive a salary.'

And of course there's Joe – sociable tonight and up for a natter, which means that he and I catch up on the latest misdemeanours of the Tory government.

We agree that the political right are currently forging the narrative, grabbing the headlines. Those of us broadly on the liberal left – progressive as we like to think we are – always thought that we were the ones in charge of the language. But no – 'wokery', 'snowflakes' and 'virtue signalling' are all clever coinages of the New Right. The GB News channel's late-night ragbag of armchair pundits are eloquent in their contempt. Unlike we 'statist socialists' or 'millennial Marxists', their bunch are the 'libertarians'. It has a good ring to it. How can anyone not be in favour of freedom?

Around this time, with Boris Johnson at risk of losing his former popularity, the press begin to talk about 'Waitrose woman' as the demography Johnson needs to woo. We are told that 'Waitrose woman' is a new type of voter reportedly identified by the Conservatives as one that Johnson has to win back, in order to hold fast at No 10. According to their research, she is 'middle class, southern and not a fan of Brexit or culture wars'. Apparently, she is also called Catherine.

'That's me!' I yelp.

A few weeks earlier, Partygate had reared its head again. First time round, the story had come and gone, with media outlets largely sympathetic to the Conservative government. But this time, there are rumblings of discontent on the Tory backbenches, to include a group of West Country MPs known as the 'Cream Tea Traitors', along with a cadre of politicians based around Melton Mowbray who are styled as the 'Pork Pie Plotters'.

I note in my diary of 13 January: 'Johnson in even more trouble as more parties emerge – positively bacchanalian. Staff falling down drunk and breaking young Wilf's swing in Downing Street garden'.

Two days later, as Carrie is reported 'hugging a friend' (when did I last hug a friend?), I add in my diary: 'How much longer can they carry on?' Of course, lots of bad jokes about 'Carrie' carrying on.

For now, both Boris and Carrie carry on. A new crisis looms a few weeks after our Burns Night, which throws all these shenanigans into perspective.

TURNING POINTS

I only speak one language
My friend at school speaks two
I wish my brain held
Two words for dog
Two worlds of sound
Two countries in one mouth
...

My friend sings two songs
And I wonder
If I will ever find another voice

From 'Language' by Amy Ludwig VanDerwater

24 February 2022

My Orchard neighbours are an international bunch – mostly bilingual, if not multilingual, outward looking, concerned with what is going on in the world beyond – particularly in mainland Europe where several of the families come from. So there is a particular interest in a major turning point early in the new year: Russia's invasion of Ukraine on 24 February. The political tittle-tattle about Partygate, the Cream Tea Traitors and Pork Pie Plotters, Operation Red Meat and Big Dog (what on earth were those all about?) now pale into insignificance. Trivial and irrelevant, along with Johnson's clever talk of 'dromedaries' and 'whack-a-mole' in the early lockdown days. Real, physical war replaces the language wars.

Armed conflict in Europe for the first time in a generation.

There are no Ukrainians at The Orchard. But there are many from countries that border Ukraine or Russia. First, of course, the Poles: Andrzej, not a resident but owner of two Orchard flats; Emil in flat fourteen; and Maggie in flat twenty; Ivan, Maggie's partner, from Bulgaria; and Anna, who is half Latvian. As well as the Hungarian family. They are fearful, sad and angry. A whole mix of emotions. Brzoska's sister Rebecca, back in Poland, has a spare room and is hosting Ukrainian nationals who are, like Brzoska and Rebecca, from the Jehovah's Witness congregation. Often, she tells me, they stay a few weeks en route to other European countries, such as Sweden. A friend in North London with a Russian wife, who is placing Ukrainian refugees into UK families, asks if I could accommodate a Ukrainian doctor and her daughter in number twelve. Reluctantly, guiltily, surveying the chaos in my one spare room, I decline.

It feels like home

It is a few days after Russia's invasion of Ukraine, and I am downstairs in flat six. Two years into Covid, we are braver about crossing thresholds, taking the first steps into unfamiliar social worlds. I have offered to babysit – as the lads are nine and twelve, we call it 'boysitting' – so that Eszter and Tamás can have a date night at the North Star down the Broadway.

Once back from the pub, Tamás and Eszter talk of the war. Both were not yet born at the time of the Hungarian invasion by Russia in 1956, though the event is deeply embedded in their recent history. I remember it, as a teenager – the same age as their son Gergő is now. He worries about family back home in Hungary, as troops mass on the borders of his country. Together, we deplore this move into a new Cold War, as I recount the optimism, excitement even, which we at Ealing Tech felt, nearly fifty years ago now, at the opportunity to teach Soviet students, when Ukraine was part of the USSR and the original Cold War was beginning to thaw.

A few weeks earlier, Eszter had talked to me one evening in my flat about how they came to The Orchard. Tamás had preceded his family in September of 2019 – he had dropped in on our annual Christmas drinks at number twelve. The later arrival of his wife and boys coincided pretty much with the arrival of Covid.

Eszter: 'We came in February 2020 and Covid came in March.'

Cathie: 'You arrived at the beginning of lockdown. You've come to a new city, you want to explore it, but suddenly you are confronted with…'

E: 'Yes, nothing! And I particularly wanted to go to Liverpool! [Eszter is a passionate Liverpool supporter.] This is my favourite country, and Liverpool is my favourite football team, and [I thought] you can buy tickets but… no you can't!'

C: 'Here you are in London, and you want to go to Liverpool, and suddenly you can't go anywhere… what was it like for you? Suddenly you're stuck at home and the children are out of school?'

E: 'It wasn't as bad as for everyone else because of the previous six months, when we had been separated. We wanted to be together again so badly that it almost felt like an opportunity – it's not a good way of putting it – but what I mean is that we could be together, without sending the kids to school. It was very hard for Balint at the beginning. For Balint the first two weeks [of school] were terrible. Not here, the present school, but the first school. He started at Manor Gardens [the first school he attended]. They were nice – it wasn't the teachers' fault, but the first two weeks he was crying, and I was crying as well, so when lockdown came, he said, "Yes, freedom!" He was very happy because he didn't have to go to school!

'I was very scared because of Covid, so it was like "please don't make me send my kids away". When Tommy went to Tesco I just – I just sanitised every item. At the beginning it was frightening but... I had my kids at home. We came here to a different country, and we had to adapt, and it was hard, but it felt like I had just got them back and I didn't have to worry because I had got them back.'

I ask Eszter what had triggered the move to London.

E: 'Actually it wasn't a plan. I wanted to come here because I was always a fan of English football and of the English language as well. So I started to learn English. Not just because of the football – though that was a strong connection.

'But Tommy – he didn't want to move from Hungary because he had a nice career, and we had a nice house. We had built our own home. Then he got the opportunity with Facebook. He came here to the UK for the interview – "OK," we agreed, "Let's see what they say, but we won't move here. Why would we? They can't offer anything." But they made him a very nice offer. So we said: "OK, let's start to think about it."

'It was a big thing. I was a Hungarian teacher – but that can't help me in England. We needed a salary for the four of us. Tommy is amazing in his field. He's a mathematician. He was a data analyst in Hungary and now he's a data engineer here in England – he was one of the best in Hungary.'

C: 'Why this part of London? Why The Orchard? Why here?'

E: 'There was a company [to help us]. We just had to tell them our priorities. OK – safe, family friendly and good schools. They said Chiswick, Hampstead and… Ealing. Chiswick and Hampstead were extremely expensive. So it was Ealing. We checked more than twenty places before The Orchard. When I entered the flats, I thought: *I want to live here*. It was just a feeling. It was bright, charming. *I want to live here…* The whole house has a… I don't know what – a soul. It's like home. We rent it, so it's not ours, but it feels like home.'

Schools for their children loom large for Eszter and Tamás. Like Basabdatta and Anirban in number eighteen, families arriving at The Orchard surf the internet to find out which are the local 'outstanding' state schools. They are likely to be pleasantly surprised. Nearly 50% of Ealing schools currently have an 'outstanding' Ofsted rating, comparing favourably with posher neighbouring boroughs. Also, for Luca and his family, Lorenzo's schooling has played a major part in their decision to stay in London for the immediate future, despite the precarity of work. Eszter and Tamás approve of the local secondary school they have chosen for Gergő. It is known for its strictness. A crooked tie earns a detention. A young man who had recently left the sister school, which shares the regime, describes it as 'Orwellian'. But it suits my friends.

Above all, Eszter wants her children to grow up in a multicultural, tolerant sort of place. She describes how her younger son Balint was so used to a monocultural, white society in Hungary that he commented on different skin colour when he first arrived in the UK.

'My son Balint – it was the first time he saw a black person in London – so he asked, "Mum, why is his skin so dark?" *OK*, I thought, *this is the time to explain that we are not all the same.*'

Towards the end of the evening, we had talked of the divisive politics in both our countries. But Eszter sees her sons' education best served for now – and indeed until the end of schooling – in London.

'I love that Balint's best friend is half Japanese. And he has a Korean friend too. Another friend is Indian. I love it and I love their stories and their culture. And I'm so happy that we can give them [their boys] a different view of life.'

Her parting shot that night is: 'I don't like this politics built on hatred. This is Orban's politics. A politics of hate. "We have to hate. We need an enemy".'

Comings and goings

After the long chat with Eszter, I had reflected on the occupants of flat six over the years. Of eighteen flats at The Orchard, number six has seen the most comings and goings.

Nancy, the Queen's hairdresser, lived out her days here. Some years later came South Africans, Brian and

Sheila McManus. Once their two daughters were born, they let out the flat and moved west to Maidenhead. Better for schools. A nicer class of person. But not before Brian, a cool, easy-going sort of chap, had helped me out in a dicey situation with the drug dealers in flat seven, next door to the McManuses. One of these, as I later realised, was doing a quick drop-off one evening, dumping the getaway car in front of my garage. I'd objected. Not a good move, as it turned out, when a threatening figure appeared on my doorstep, claiming that, in the effort to move my Nissan Micra, I'd clipped his Mercedes. Brian, great at pouring oil on troubled waters, had neatly stepped in.

'Look, Cathie is saying you're within your rights – she may have scratched your car. How about exchanging telephone numbers? I'm sure you both have insurance, and we can come to some agreement?'

At the thought of more public attention, my guy departed pretty swiftly. Tranquillity was restored on the ground floor. And the troupe of number six residents continued. For a time, there was the charming Iranian couple with their son Bassam. I didn't get to know them well but always wished I had. I would have liked to know more about why they left Iran, almost certainly as political refugees, whether they planned to return, what their plans were for Bassam, clearly a talented boy. Until suddenly, they were gone. The Iranian family were replaced by a rather unpleasant pair of sisters who left accusatory notices on the stairwell out the back, of the kind, 'Will the person who stole my mobile phone kindly return it'. Very un-Orchard. And no one had stolen the phone. Then the two sets of twins: the precocious twin girls followed the two teenagers, the sons of Len and Joan.

Much later, two more boys, not twins this time, Olly and Matt, children of the lovely bohemian photographers. And finally, the Wild Girls. Delightful. They turned into howling werewolves only on the 'full moon' party nights. Perfect citizens by day. Highly respected young schoolteachers.

And now Eszter, Tamás and their boys.

Boysitting

I start to pay closer attention to family life in flat six on my boysitting evenings. The original thirties fireplace of Nancy's era remains but is concealed by a giant TV screen. Never on when I visit. Conversation is respected, along with attention to adults in this household. Eszter's boys are well disciplined, with bath time and bedtimes scrupulously adhered to. Once in bed, they can read for as long as they want to. Earlier in the evening, we play old-fashioned games: a Hungarian version of I-spy and Snap and Pick Up Sticks, which Balint loves. Gergő teaches me poker. Then bilingual Scrabble. Balint starts to giggle nervously as the word GAY is offered in our Scrabble game. Somewhere he's picked up the negative connotation – perhaps as overheard in playground bullying.

'No, it's not a bad word,' I say. 'It has two meanings in English – both good.'

And we talk. I ask them about the major turning point in their own lives, before lockdown, before the recent war in Ukraine. It would seem obvious that the big transition for Gergő and Balint was their parents' choice, rather spur of the moment, to up and leave the place where they were born and grew up. A new country, new schooling. Above all, a new language.

A squirrel at the window

And then, to cap it all, a wholly new way of life. Being locked up – or rather locked down. But no, what Gergő wants to begin with is – not the trauma of leaving his home country, nor being socially isolated and away from school for months, not having to communicate in English, but – squirrels. The Orchard squirrels, he insists, are special.

Gergő: 'What was really amazing is that the squirrels come up to the window and eat out of your hands! That's amazing. That would never happen in Hungary.'

Cathie: 'That's interesting. I would never have thought of that. I know that Hanna next door – she always fed the squirrels. Maybe that's why the squirrels became so tame. But you liked that?'

G: 'I liked that!'

Gergő also raises the preoccupation that universally affects arrivals in a new country: food.

'The food here in England is… let's just say it's terrible!' We laugh.

'OK, you've got fish and chips, and that's nice, but it's not the same as the cuisine in Hungary or Poland. I mean, yeah, that's one thing I miss.'

Gergő reserves his deepest scorn for the bread.

'The bread! Here in England if you want bread you will get these little soggy squares... and it's kind of depressing, looking at these little slices of bread – of square bread without fresh crusts that have been sitting on the shelf for I don't know how long – a week or so – compared to the fresh bread that you can find five hundred metres away from your house in Hungary.'

Becoming bilingual

A major transition in the lives of Balint and Gergő is becoming bilingual. In Hungary, theirs was a monolingual world. Learning a second language is a challenge but also culturally and cognitively enriching – a number of research studies support this view. Now Balint and Gergő have a comfortable command of two languages.

I am intrigued by the boys' proficiency in English. Their fluency and expressiveness is exceptional. As a former English language teacher, I expect the learning of English to be absorbed from peers, schooling, sometimes specific English language instruction. Local schools in Ealing have long supported bilingualism in a number of ways. Gergő acknowledges that this was organised during the few weeks at his primary school before lockdown descended.

G: 'I had a really nice teacher. What she did – instead of teaching like with the "normal" children – she didn't give me the hard subjects so that I had no idea what to do. She didn't straight up tell me to "write a story about a fictional character". She sent me to the back of the room with other children who had recently arrived in the school. There were like two other children.'

C: 'New arrivals?'

G: 'One of them was Japanese. One of them was from Yemen – he was Yemeni. And there was another one. We learnt together at the back of the class. We were like our own little community... my teacher would give us sheets, translated into our own language. Uwi would get it in Japanese, Mamoon would get it in... I don't know what language they speak in Yemen. They would all get that, and they would all get the same sheet in English.'

C: 'You new arrivals could all read in your own language?'

G: 'Yes, we got an English sheet and we got a translation sheet.'

C: 'They must have had a teacher who spoke your language? Hungarian and er...?'

G: 'They might have used Google Translate.'

Despite efforts made by the boys' schools, it becomes clear that – particularly during lockdown – Gergő and Balint learnt most of their English at home with Eszter. Also, as Gergő points out, their English language learning was strongly supported by literacy. 'We learnt English on paper,' as Gergő puts it.

C: 'The interesting thing with both of you is that your vocabulary is good and your grammar is good. You make few mistakes with the structure and the grammar.'

G: 'This is because we both learnt English on paper, so we don't hear it like people who grow up in England. When they are babies... for instance, it's breakfast – they are having breakfast – and then of course they think: *breakfast*. They know this word because they see they are having breakfast. But then they need to learn how to spell. However, we straight off hear how to spell it, because we didn't just hear it but we *read* it on a piece of paper.'

C: 'Yes, you didn't learn just by speaking, you always had the written word to reinforce the language, to "bring it home"; you hear "breakfast" and then you see it and that reinforces it?'

G: 'I think we learnt reading before speaking English.'

C: 'Was this back in Hungary or here?'

G: 'I didn't have a lot of English in Hungary so we're talking about *here*.'

At the time of this conversation, Gergő and Balint had been learning English for about three years, much of the time, due to lockdown constraints, at home with their mother.

The elephant in the room

Flat six, not quite home, though comfortable and warm. The spartan, makeshift look of a rented flat. An outdoor family, so lots of waterproof jackets and wellingtons in the hall. A world away from Nancy's time in number six, where the family sitting room would boast glass-fronted cabinets with their cherished ornaments and family trophies. I'm thinking of my Uncle Tom and Auntie Annie's council house in Greenock, more modest than Nancy's place, but the same idea: a handful of books, what we used to call 'knick-knacks', a set of cheap encyclopaedias. Always the *Reader's Digest*.

Gergő becomes fascinated by the similarities between our Orchard flats, the funny fanlights over some of the doors. But not others. He notices oddities I've lived with for years and barely remarked. Nothing escapes Gergő's gaze. One is the matter of the brass bells, one on my living room wall, a second in my bedroom. Suggestive of a time when the flats were service flats perhaps. Long before my time. But, in number twelve at least – it seems not in the other flats – the bells have always been there.

When compared to the anonymity of number six, every artefact in my place is dense with memories: travel, family, old friends, lovers. Few of these objects have any value, other than sentimental: an old cigar tin, skeletons of saguaro cactus taken, illegally, from the Arizona desert, stones and shells from long-forgotten beaches, a tiny vase, which my old friend Carole Simons retrieved, as a memento for me, from her parents' flat in Golders Green after they died. I loved her father and the Jewish jokes he told. The one I always remember is perhaps not even particularly Jewish.

'He could always hold his own,' I said, about a mutual acquaintance.

'Well, he'd look funny holding anyone else's,' said Philip Simons.

The stories that are embedded in the things scattered around my flat have significance only to me. My friend Una is a more serious collector, her small cottage in Cambridgeshire stuffed to overflowing with curios from childhood and beyond. Some are wildly politically incorrect, like her collection of gollywogs, kept since she was a girl. The newest arrival is a giant stuffed tiger she picked up for a fiver, not from her trip to Nepal but from a local charity shop. Terrifying when, groping for the loo, you bump into him in the middle of the night.

'Who will want him when I'm gone?' Una says, wistfully.

My own most recent acquisition in number twelve, and one especially admired by Simone, is an elephant. Originally it was a lamp stand, one of a pair in Auntie Annie's living room, which Tom, her sea-going husband, brought back from India. My cousin Bill and I shared a childhood love for the beasts. Angus and Morag I called them. Bill captured Morag on Auntie Annie's death. She still has pride of place in his family living room in Wemyss Bay in western Scotland. But for years, Angus went missing, until my cousin Kathleen, Annie's daughter, stumbled across him in her attic in Stranraer.

Quite recently, an ungainly package landed on my doorstep at The Orchard. Over the decades in Kathleen's attic, poor Angus had lost his tusks as well as the frilly fifties lampshade, balanced on his trunk. He now stands in my living room, a new lampshade perched jauntily on his trunk. I have placed him on that crudely built pine table in the corner, one of my dad's less successful carpentry efforts. Companionless, long parted from Morag.

Of course, I call him the elephant in the room.

Election day in Hungary

A few weeks later, it is election day in Hungary, and Eszter and her family are in Budapest, in order to register their vote. She sends an email in the morning:

> *We have done what we must have done, voted AGAINST Orban! I'm afraid it won't be enough because there are loads of brainwashed people. I am nervous, I would be devastated if Orban won again... please keep your fingers crossed for the democracy in Hungary!*

By evening, the results are bad – for liberals and democrats everywhere. Another email from Eszter:

The results: the death of democracy. I am glad to have a chance to live somewhere else and give a better life to my kids... it's hard to accept – Hungary was a beautiful and valuable country but the vast majority is dumber than I could imagine.

THE LAST CAKE

The corridor became a new space
For Christmas and parties and masks – just in case –
But mainly for gossip, cocktails and champagne.
You were there for it all, in sunshine and rain.
And yes – best of all – for God's sake
Was the cake!

From 'Leaving Song for Bart and Emma and Darius the Dog',

Cathie Wallace

September 2022

The Covid era is slowly receding. There was an odd comfort in that withdrawal from everyday life. The retreat from threat, the reduced sight of the world through the keyhole. Now we are pretty much 'out there' again. The Arboretum has an air of back to normal. Two tiny girls, with remarkable agility, are scaling that pretty tree in the middle of the park, not an adult in sight. They look like giant butterflies, one in a blue frock, one in yellow. As I watch, they climb higher and higher. I love their abandonment, the sense of freedom.

Still, post-Covid, things will not be the same. Not

Plaque for Darius

in the wider world and not closer to home. OK, we have stopped sanitising the vegetables, mask wearing has eased up and friends may risk a quick hug, but there is still caution. Also, the need for a bit of playfulness. The now yearly Christmas ritual at The Orchard of decorating the Serbian spruce, in the foyer. The plaque on the wall of the corridor, just by the entrance door, dedicated to Darius, famous dog actor. No, Darius hasn't died – that story comes later.

Covid departs, but not before leaving a sting in the tale, by which many folk in The Orchard finally get the damn thing. Including myself. Not badly, a tickle in the throat, but it has meant missing a planned trip to Ireland to flaunt my newly acquired Irish passport, as well as my friend's wedding in Wales. Getting married for the first time at the age of seventy.

'See the Covid infection as a rite of passage,' says Jennifer, who has, similarly, been mildly afflicted. I isolate dutifully. More time to note the persisting, small adjustments to daily life, conversations, behaviour that would hitherto have passed unobserved, to see the formerly familiar 'with fresh eyes', as the anthropologists say. Children – largely absent in the early days – are one Orchard change, some boisterous like young Clara, some, like the Virt boys downstairs, so quiet I have to consciously remember their presence. Perfect neighbours, and now friends.

The Old-Timers and the New Cosmopolitans

In recent years, The Orchard has witnessed the coming and going that typifies modern times. Those who have become friends leave, and the stranger arrives. As Tolstoy said, 'All great literature is one of two stories; a man goes on a journey or a stranger comes to town'.

Eszter and her family, as New Cosmopolitans, are not – yet – leaving for good. But – once freed from the constraints of Covid and when school is out – they pack the kids in the car and take off to Scotland, Wales, the Lake District, France, Spain, Portugal and of course Hungary. Tamás can work anywhere – currently for Facebook – he is not geographically confined. Eszter less so. She has had to compromise, with a less-than-ideal job as a school meals assistant in an Ealing school.

With Viktor Orban firmly in place – a mini-Putin, says Eszter – the family may never return to live in Hungary. Liverpool, home of Eszter's much-loved football team, could be the future. Great people, a liberal city and cheaper to buy a place than financially out-of-reach London.

Back in the eighties and nineties during my early Orchard years, my neighbours largely stayed put. There were hints of earlier adventurous lives: hairdresser Nancy accompanied the Queen on her Commonwealth visit to Kenya in February 1952, the one where she learnt of her father's death. Gerald had lived in Egypt and Africa and, of course, there was the dramatic sprint to Lake Victoria, as reported by his friend Andrzej, to carry an urgent wartime missive.

Many Old-Timer stories remain untold, unverified or under wraps. Over the years, there have been minor tiffs, territorial disputes, rumoured affairs, often thwarted – more *Brief Encounter* than *Fatal Attraction*. A few folk, like Gerald and Claudine, were travellers, but sedately and in comfort I always imagine, nothing like Emil's frantic dash across continents or war zones. Nor the impromptu flight of Bart and Emma, during a pause in Covid constraints, to get married in the Elvis Presley suite in Las Vegas.

What would the Old-Timers have thought of it all? Brexit, Covid and now war in Europe? They had experienced the Second World War. More than that, several had seen active service. Would they have been seduced by the Boris Johnson narrative, the Churchillian tribute act? Recalling Hulda's sharp wit and clear-sightedness about so many things, it seems unlikely. She and Dack and other Orchardians were traditional Tories, sticklers for propriety and, dare I say it, the truth.

Lots of different stories

The Old-Timers were very much of *here*. Very English? suggests Eszter, as I try one day to find the right word. I hesitate to say 'white', though they were, more that they were culturally and socially homogenous, sharing the same assumptions and values.

The same stories to make sense of their lives.

Until recently, 'being British' was a pretty clear-cut affair. To do with being an island nation? Solid institutions, which have been around forever, like Parliament and the monarchy? Who knows? But for many of my newer Orchard neighbours, a more tentative identity and the uncertainty of boundaries is part of their history. Latvia, the home of Anna's father, was part of the Soviet Union before the war. From 1795 to 1918, Poland was split between Prussia, the Habsburg monarchy, and Russia and had no independent existence. And Hungary, once a dual monarchy with Austria in the Austro-Hungarian Empire had, by 1920, lost two thirds of its territory. Nearly one third of the ten million ethnic Hungarians found themselves resident outside their diminished homeland, many in Romania where they live today, largely in a region known as Transylvania. Eszter fills in some of the detail.

'You know Hungary is very small, but it used to be very big. Until the First World War, we had a very big country with Transylvania – think of vampires! In 1940, Northern Transylvania reverted to Hungary, but then after the end of the Second World War, it went back to Romania. What was the most eastern part of Hungary is now in Romania but populated by Hungarians. We went there almost every summer to collect data. [Eszter's father was an anthropologist.] And this was my childhood. It has got a very ancient Hungarian culture and – because they are isolated – they have kept their own culture.'

They have 'kept their own culture', says Eszter, at first glance an attractive thought. And yet it flies in the face of the cultural mixing valued by Eszter and many Orchardians – values that favour multiculturalism over a single monolithic culture. On the night of the Robert Burns celebration a few weeks earlier, Ivan had suggested that we turn the discourse around, so that 'monoculture' becomes the marked term, the one out of kilter with contemporary life: it is *multiculture*, said Ivan, that is our natural habitat. We had all nodded in approval.

Perhaps what Ivan means is that thinking multiculturally allows us to question what is taken for granted, to gain distance from our own presuppositions and prejudices. Often younger, more diverse in social background, nationality and ethnicity, the people I'm calling the New Cosmopolitans seem more readily to take this on board. Gergő says one day, talking about how much he feels he gains from the diversity of his Ealing schoolmates' life experience:

'They have lots of different stories. They share their viewpoints. Let's say in Hungary, you would probably get just the *Hungarian* point of things: there would be one common viewpoint. But here, at my school, you're gonna hear different stories from all of them. They're going to educate you. It kind of makes you a better person.'

An octopus with eight hands
If, for people like Eszter and her family, multiculturalism and diversity is to be willingly embraced – or rather 'just the way things are' – other strands of contemporary life cause immediate day-to-day headaches for some of my Orchard neighbours. Getting and keeping a job is one.

In times of job deregulation, people, many of whom have come to the UK specifically to find work, need to be sure-footed, nimble in picking up opportunities, however insecure. Emma and I talk about Bart, a talented writer and actor:

Cathie: 'I know he does stunt work but he does a lot more too.'

Emma: 'He's a thespian trained actor.'

C: 'He's a proper actor.'

E: 'He's a proper actor. He'll work doing whatever he can get work for, but yes, a proper actor.'

Identity matters – more than ever in precarious times. Yes, Bart will turn his hand to anything, but as Emma says firmly, 'He is a proper actor.' He has been to drama school. Eszter, though currently working as a school meals assistant, is a 'proper teacher', trained as a teacher of Hungarian. Luca talks about how, having trained to be a skilled baker, lockdown employment practices have meant his being positioned as a jack of all trades. Nonetheless, he insists, 'I am a baker.'

Luca: 'And every time this is what they tell me: "No, I cannot give a you pay rise." I say, "I did all the training to be a baker; I'm doing everything. I don't know what I can do more than this – be an octopus with eight hands?" I worked alone by myself for so long, particularly at the weekend. It was impossible. This was before lockdown. Then they start to ask me, because lockdown is coming, they start to ask me – do the coffees, bring the things to the customer, and I say, "I am sorry, I did all the training to be a *baker*."

'In theory, I *am* a baker, but I'm not *paid* as a baker… you ask me to be coffee maker, waiter.'

People like Luca and Bart need to have more than one string to their bow. Academics have described this as the age of 'fast capitalism'. It is certainly capitalism, and it is pretty 'fast': one minute Luca is 'a proper baker', the next – as he says – 'a coffee maker, a waiter' – an octopus with eight hands.

Queens

Despite all the uncertainties around Covid, the war in Ukraine, British and Hungarian politics and the state of the world more widely, we've tried to keep the merriment going. Any excuse for a party. Hungarian goulash for Luca and his little ménage when they move on to a bigger place, just opposite Ealing Hospital. A summer barbecue inviting Basabdatta, Anirban and Arin, who've now bought a flat just round the corner but are still honorary Orchardians. They have been replaced in flat eighteen by Robbie and Jill. They seem to favour their anglicised names, although Robbie is from Peru and Jill, who met Robbie in the UK, came here as a student from mainland China. Jill is ambitious for her kids, teenagers Alberto and Sandro. On her own admission, she is a bit of a tiger mother. A piano has been installed upstairs, the daily plodding rendition of classic tunes, always after school at five o'clock, suggesting aspiration rather than talent.

It is 11 September, a few days after a momentous event for all of us: the death of Queen Elizabeth. We feel that we have to mark the occasion. After all, as soon as they heard the news of the Queen's passing on their radios, more than fifty black cab drivers had driven directly to The Mall to line the road leading to Buckingham Palace as a tribute to the monarch. Closer to home, St Peter's Church, just round the corner, was hosting a 'Pimm's and Hymns' event.

This is not quite for us. Still, wishing to celebrate Elizabeth's longevity and the undoubted love and respect most of us held for her, we plump for gin and Dubonnet in the garden. Apparently, this was a favourite tipple both for the Queen Mother in her day and the Queen herself. Known for her modest taste and lifestyle (the Queen 'only had two G and Ds a day', we are told), it's easy to forget that this involves a double shot of strong alcohol. After our garden carousing, Eszter, who rarely drinks, is sloshed for days.

It had been an eventful week. A new prime minister, Liz Truss, replacing the now disgraced Boris Johnson, crowned by a mere handful of Tories and, just days later, a new king. Young Balint, distraught at the Queen's death, is not at all impressed with the idea of a king. Kings don't have the mystique, the magic of queens. Balint, just nine years old, has even worked out the order of succession so that we might have a queen again, a proper queen, not a consort (no disrespect to Camilla). This might (just) happen within Balint's lifetime, as long as the intervening kings – Charles, William and George – do not live for an inconveniently long period of time. Also, of course, that George's firstborn is a girl.

Queens have always had a particular kind of power. The great queens of history, Elizabeth I, Catherine II of Russia, as well as our own Elizabeth II. Queen bees. Ealing itself – Queen of the Suburbs.

I recall in the early Orchard days trying to explain to my five-year-old niece Claire how we came to have two women running the country. The role of Queen Elizabeth was clear to her, but not that of Margaret Thatcher, our first female prime minister, at the time quite recently elected. Claire called her 'Queen Thatcher'. Sceptical about the role of two powerful women in public life and snorting with contempt she said, 'You cannot have two queens!'

Now it's King Charles III. I am the only person, apart from Joe maybe, at The Orchard who remembers the death of the last king. I was a pupil at Culcheth Primary School. The teacher came into class and asked us all to stand up. 'The King is dead.' The girl next to me said, 'You've gone all pale.' Testimony to the power of monarchy, even when we don't believe in it. Even as a nine-year-old, I'm not sure I did.

Despite strong Republican sentiment at The Orchard, not counting Balint of course, some of us are wondering what to do about Charles's coronation on 6 May 2023. It seems churlish to bypass another excuse for a party.

I survey the scene outside. The Orchard garden furniture is old and tatty. My friend Ruth's green iron table and two chairs, a bequest to me when, at the age of forty, she knew she was dying, have been at The Orchard as long as I have. They must stay, for sentimental, if not practical, reasons. And also, Kim's seat. Perhaps a new bench? I google the possibilities. We are not really into patio furniture sets, 'which add dining and lounging elegance to your garden', nor 'two-seater bistro sets'. Not even 'a beautiful hand-finished carved Union Jack teak bench, which includes the new royal crest of King Charles'.

I abandon the quest, especially as the unpredictability of an English spring may not allow for garden celebrations. We may end up with Coronation Cake in the Corridor.

We go ahead with the coronation high jinks, but in our own way, allowing some of us to do it ironically. Joe doesn't show up at all, however. Later, when I bump into him with the greeting, 'we missed you, Joe', he says, 'I won't celebrate repressive regimes.'

Cake

Cake has loomed large in lockdown. Cake as baking – doing something practical – learning a new skill, always a good idea; cake as a gift: an offering to others. Above all, cake as therapy, as comfort. We even had the new coinage 'cakeism' to describe Prime Minister Johnson's 'have your cake and eat it' lockdown philosophy: the notion that it is possible to govern without making hard choices ('Boris Johnson, "cakeism" and the Blitz spirit', Gideon Rachman, *Financial Times*, 15 July 2019). Rachman warns, presciently, that Johnson might 'risk ending up as a British version of Marie Antoinette – a French queen, infamous for an ill-advised remark about cake, who met a sticky end'.

But the cake discourse continued. There was the famous birthday cake at the controversial 'was it a party or not' occasion of Boris Johnson's birthday in 2020. In other words, was Johnson aware or not that an at-the-time 'illegal' party was going on? Two years later, Johnson's supporters continue to lament that 'he was just dismissed over cake'.

Stoical Orchardians do not subscribe to cakeism: having our cake and eating it is quite definitely not for us. But we love cake. Or rather the *idea* of cake, and in the absence of any Covid pretext, we want to keep the corridor cake going. It's Emil's birthday again. The way time has worked over the last few years remains unnerving, and I can hardly believe another year has passed. On this occasion, Emil's birthday coincides with the brief, barely believable 'blink and you missed it' Liz Truss prime ministership. Leading me to comment on Emil's invitation that, after my weekly Bookbreak class in Ladbroke Grove – the one I run with Ian on reading with depressed people in the community – I'll need cake.

Emil says, 'Post the election of Truss, you'll need half of Wembley Stadium to accommodate depressed people in the community.'

Emil's mum Barbara joins our little gathering in the corridor, in pearls and elegant black, as if off to the dress circle at Covent Garden. She looks magnificent.

In truth, the apple cake from the Polish bakers Soya

down the Broadway – a favourite of Emil's – is tastier, but it cannot compete decoratively with the grand affair that Barbara has ordered on the internet. Aesthetically impressive but gastronomically disappointing. I hide my portion of the Mad Hatter's cake behind *War and Peace* in the corridor bookcase, to be retrieved later.

I am minded of that party all those years ago – the arrival party organised by Jill and Douglas Appleby, who were leaving flat twelve, as I took over. Also ten people. But no thoughts of corridor goings-on in those days. Comfy in my sitting room. Some of the new Orchard people make up the numbers on this occasion, especially the glamorous Australian Kristina Kellaway. But there are important absences. Emma, Bart and Darius have gone. A few weeks earlier, they had left for the United States.

Emma, Bart and Darius go to Chicago

Bart, Emma and Darius have brightened our lives and shared the Covid years. Their relentless optimism was catching. Now they are off. Archetypal cosmopolitans, they are setting up in Chicago. Bart has an agent, Emma a new, high-powered job as Chief Marketing Director for a pharmaceutical firm. Darius is already booked on the flight.

Not long before they leave, Emma describes how they came to be 'nomads', eventually making the decision to come to London:

'And we just said, "OK, yes, let's do this." We'd done the move before from our home city Adelaide to Sydney. But this is very, very different – moving overseas and literally to the other side of the world. All the personal connections that you leave behind. So yes, we thought about that. But at the same time we thought, you know, we need to pursue our own lives.

This feels like a really interesting, exciting thing to do. So my work was the vehicle for us getting here. So yes, it wasn't really thought of for too long. We just said, "Yeah, let's do it.'"

She demurs when I use the term 'cosmopolitan'. Too fancy. 'We just went for it,' she says.

Emma: 'You know what. Bart and I are like nomads. We don't really have an anchor to a city, to a country, to anything. We're just kind of going with the flow.'

Cathie: 'You are cosmopolitans, citizens of the world.'

E: 'We are now. I don't think it was what we had intended. But as I say, we are "yes" people. If it feels positive… you can quickly do the pros and cons, the calculations. You know, let's do it.'

C: 'I think this was typified by the fact that you went to Las Vegas to get married—'

E: 'We kept that all very private as well. Surprise! It was just something that we wanted to do. A little bit of light in the darkness that we'd all lived through with Covid. Again, why not? Let's do it.'

Unlike the earlier, more settled community, the New Cosmopolitans, often renting rather than buying, don't expect to stay long. Bart and Emma had originally planned – as far as they planned anything – for about three years. Emma describes coming upon The Orchard. It is a story that echoes Eszter's first impressions but also my own experience, nearly forty years earlier as I approached number twelve, the twin of number eleven, with front doors side by side, facing that intimidatingly long corridor. My impression that day was also of light and sun, and greenness.

Emma: 'We looked at so many apartments, and in the end, I remember I was at my wits' end. And Bart was travelling for pantomime, so I was looking at houses on my own, and the real estate agent pulled up to The Orchard. And I thought, *this is interesting*.'

Cathie: 'What did you think when you saw that funny canopy?'

E: 'Almost like a hotel… I just didn't really know what to make of it. Looks like an old school. Or a hotel. I couldn't quite…'

C: 'Not a very glamorous hotel. A dingy hotel.'

E: 'OK, it didn't look promising, but be open-minded, I said, because really I'd seen so many properties and was becoming quite desperate. And walking along, opening up the front door, walking down the very art deco corridor up the stairs. OK, very interesting.

'Then literally – I just opened the door to flat eleven. It was just a little oasis – it was sun-drenched; it was bright; it was leafy, because it was on the first floor. And I just thought, *wow!* There was no furniture in there at all, so I got a real sense of the space. And I was taken with it immediately. And I hadn't met anyone at The Orchard at all, and so we didn't know what we were walking into, who our neighbours would be. But I just loved the apartment. I loved that it felt quite private.

'Yeah, let's do it.'

A final ode
The departure of Emma, Bart and the dog Darius produced one last ode:

Leaving Song for Bart and Emma and Darius the Dog

This talented trio
Are brimming with brio,
Santa jackets and hats, yoga mats
For the fit and the brave out the back
On the grass, tits over arse.
Or is it the other way round?
Whatever the case, we all found
You such fun – the excitement you brought,
If at times overwrought!

The corridor became a new space
For Christmas and parties and masks – just in case –
But mainly for gossip, cocktails and champagne.
You were there for it all, in sunshine and rain.
You brought joy; you brought fun,
E'en if overdone – just a tad –
When things got crazy, even quite mad:
Catherine wheels at New Year,
When you almost set fire to that house, so I hear.

Across the way

I still cannot believe they are gone. That their light is not on across the way, out the back stairs.

A new family – John and Edith, with an older couple, Edith's parents – has arrived in number eleven. They are part of the British National (Overseas) programme, set up specifically for Hong Kongers, wishing to escape an increasingly repressive China-led regime, overseen by a hawkish Xi Jinping.

John and I risk a warm but awkward Covid handshake.

'And how long have you been here?'

'Forty years.'

EPILOGUE:
THEY HAVE GONE

ASTROFF

They have gone! The professor, I suppose, is glad to go. He couldn't be tempted back now by a fortune.

MARINA comes in.

MARINA

They have gone. [She sits down in an armchair and knits her stocking.]

SONIA comes in wiping her eyes.

SONIA

They have gone. God be with them. [To her uncle] And now, Uncle Vanya, let us do something!

VOITSKI

To work! To work!

SONIA

It is long, long, since you and I have sat together at this table. [She lights a lamp on the table] No ink! [She takes the inkstand to the cupboard and fills it from an ink bottle] How sad it is to see them go!

MME. VOITSKAYA comes slowly in.
MME. VOITSKAYA
They have gone.

Act four, *Uncle Vanya* by Anton Chekhov

Uncle Vanya is a story about those who leave and those who stay. At the end of the play, four of the characters – those who stay – echo the line 'they have gone'. They then quietly, stoically, resume their lives.

Sometimes I envisage a Chekhovian end to our Orchard stories. *The Cherry Orchard* has obvious resonance. We too have lost our trees, the wild beauty of earlier days and are facing turbulent social change.

Still, I favour the link with *Uncle Vanya*, my favourite Chekhov play. The corridors empty, the partying long forgotten. Bart, Emma and Darius – ghosts. Joining the older ghosts of schoolteacher Saoirse O'Brien, playwright Noel Greig, the old soldiers Jan and Gerald, the gardeners such as Dack, as on that first idyllic spring morning when I first set eyes on The Orchard. Kim of course. Having a quick fag and a cuppa in his shed.

The Vanya analogy with Orchard folk cannot be pushed too far. Professor Serebrakoff and his beautiful wife Helena are heading back to the city. The longing is always for Moscow or Leningrad. At The Orchard, those of us staying are city folk, at best suburban. Those leaving are off to calmer, rural pastures, as well as to exotic lands further afield. A few days earlier, Hanna, finding me in contemplative mood in the garden, had come to tell me that she and Ziggy were moving on, west, to Cookham. Others will follow.

James and Simone will fly off to a life, uncertain yet full of promise, in Zambia.

Once Balint and Gergő are out of school, Eszter and Tamás will flee too, maybe to Liverpool, so that Eszter can be near her beloved football team.

Joe might finally take the still unpacked suitcases to Manchester to join his brother and niece. Or maybe go back to the Australian skies he loves.

Leaving myself and Emil.

Sitting over our favourite Irish whisky in the garden…

They have gone.

They have gone.

SELECTED REFERENCES

Debjani Chatterjee, 2003 'Interlude' in *Poems for The Waiting Rooms of the National Health Service,* NHS, The Poetry Society and Arts Council of Great Britain

Anton Chekhov, 1897 'Uncle Vanya' in *Chekhov Plays.* Penguin Classics

Damon Galgut, 2021 *The Promise.* Chatto and Windus

Jackie Kay, 2017 'Planet Farage' in *Bantam.* Picador Poetry

Paul Howard Lang and Dr Jonathan Oates 2021, *Secret Ealing.* Amberley Publishing.

Vladimir Lenin, 2003 New Edition *Essential Works of Lenin What is to be done and other writings.* Dover Publications

Doris Lessing, 1976 *The Memoirs of a Survivor.* Picador

Cho Nam-Joo, 2020 *Kim Jiyoung, Born 1982.* Simon and Schuster

Mary Oliver, 2003 'Wild Geese' in *Owls and Other Fantasies.* Beacon Press, Boston

Catherine Slessor 2020, 'Corridors of uncertainty: Modernist utopia and cinematic menace'. The Architectural Review

Barton Williams 2018 *But What Are You?.* Olympia Publishers

Benjamin Zephaniah, 2015 'Neighbours' *Best Poems Encyclopedia*

ACKNOWLEDGEMENTS

I should like to thank all my Orchard friends and neighbours who so generously supported the writing of this book. Particular thanks are due to Min Dinning, Lynn Fairley-Rose and Lynn Scrivener, who commented in detail on the text. I am also indebted to those who read earlier drafts of this work. They are Alison Appleby, Elsa Auerbach, John Clegg, Melanie Cooke, David Gordon, Frances and Alan King, Emil Kowalski, Tom Langham, Marilyn Martin-Jones, Monica Mulenga, Barbara Sinclair, Marek and Teresa Stella-Sawicki, Nicky Walker, Andrew Ward and Sue Wright.

This book is printed on paper from sustainable sources managed under the Forest Stewardship Council (FSC) scheme.

It has been printed in the UK to reduce transportation miles and their impact upon the environment.

For every new title that Troubador publishes, we plant a tree to offset CO_2, partnering with the More Trees scheme.

For more about how Troubador offsets its environmental impact, see www.troubador.co.uk/sustainability-and-community